Parenting a Child with *Special* Needs

Parenting a Child with Special Needs

ROSEMARIE S. COOK

ZondervanPublishingHouse
Grand Rapids, Michigan

A Division of HarperCollinsPublishers

Parenting a Child with Special Needs
Copyright © 1992 by Rosemarie S. Cook, Ph.D.

Requests for information should be addressed to:
Zondervan Publishing House
Grand Rapids, Michigan 49530

Library of Congress Cataloging-in-Publication Data

Cook, Rosemarie S.
 Parenting a child with special needs / Rosemarie S. Cook
  p. cm.
 Includes bibliographical references and index.
 ISBN 0-310-58551-1 (pbk.)
  1. Parents of handicapped children—United States. 2. Parenting
 —Religious aspects—Christianity. I. Title.
HQ759.913.C66   1992
649'.151—dc20   92-21726
                                                     CIP

Some of the names in this book have been changed to protect the privacy of the families described.

Edited by Linda Vanderzalm
Cover design by Jack Foster

Printed in the United States of America

92 93 94 95 96 97 / EP / 10 9 8 7 6 5 4 3 2 1

To my four sons, Jimmy, Chris, Steve, and Shawn:

As each of you grows and matures,
may you be aware that
"There is a time for everything,
and a season for every activity
under heaven" (Eccl. 3:1).

May you know God's grace, peace, and love
in all the seasons of your lives.

Mom

CONTENTS

PART IV
MAKING PEACE WITH THE SITUATION

ACKNOWLEDGMENTS

Thank you to those family members, friends, students, and colleagues who supported me with words of encouragement and with prayer through the months of writing this book. Your names are too many to list, but I thank God for each one of you.

Special thanks to Christina Gershon, who, as my graduate assistant, helped with research, references, and compilation of materials. Also thank you to Lynnette Watson, who, while managing to keep up with all the other demands of being a faculty secretary, took time to work on the computer to help me meet my deadlines.

Thanks are also due to those parents who participated in the research project, giving of their time to share their stories of dying and rising, never an easy process.

INTRODUCTION

On a recent Sunday morning, during a quiet time in the church service, I heard a low-toned muttering that sounded familiar. During communion, as the congregation processed forward to receive the Eucharistic bread and to drink from the cup, I saw Charlie. My guess had been accurate—he was present, worshiping with us, and interjecting his own form of prayer in our liturgy.

Charlie, in his thirties, lives in an apartment a few miles from our church. His parents have retired and moved south. Worshiping with us is important to Charlie, and he comes on most Sundays. Charlie has a job and lives in a supervised residence. He always dresses appropriately for church, although not flawlessly. His shirt is often not tucked in all the way around, but that doesn't matter. What counts is that he is part of our church body and is welcomed by us.

On the other side of the church on that Sunday, in between his parents, sat eleven-year-old Andrew. His helper dog, Sandy, snoozed under the pew, which is her usual church style, and Andrew's wheelchair was parked in the aisle. Andrew attends public school, and Sandy carries his books and necessities in her own blue backpack. Andrew won't be in church for the next month or so; he is going to a medical center a hundred miles away to receive therapy and work on his independence skills.

Andrew and Charlie provided me with a lot of material for reflection that Sunday, particularly because the Gospel and subsequent homily was about the story of the talents. Even though the biblical talent is usually thought of as money, the focus that Sunday was on the talents as individual giftedness, which we must develop.

I thought about the talents of Andrew and Charlie, with contrasting disabilities and differing gifts. I considered our own sons, each with gifts in specific areas. And I thought about Chris.

Chris is our second son, and because of Chris's impact on my life and the life of my family, I can write this book. Chris lives with disabilities, and those disabilities limit his life. At age twenty-five, he can't understand the simplest addition problem. He can't drive a car and will never have a checking account. He may not know what to do in case of an emergency, and he can't place a phone call. He will always need someone to tell him what clothes are appropriate to wear for the occasion and the weather. He will always need someone to help him manage money, buy clothes, maintain his health habits, and prepare his food.

But Chris also has gifts. Chris possesses a sense of peace that communicates that he's happy being who he is. He smiles often and lets people know how much he enjoys their company. He's enthusiastic about sports and music both as participant and observer. He's sensitive to people's moods and will empathize with whatever a person is feeling. He enters into prayer and worship with his whole being.

If you've decided to read this book, you probably have or are close to a child with a disability or some sort of special need. Maybe your child has a physical disability, like spina bifida, cerebral palsy, or blindness. Maybe your child has mental impairments, from mild learning disabilities to severe developmental retardation. Or maybe your child has several disabilities that limit his or her life.

Disabilities vary greatly from person to person. For the purposes of this book, let's define *disability* as any condition that "requires significant or extraordinary . . . assistance or adaptation in order for a person to perform the tasks of daily living."[1] Children with special needs can best be described by the term "developmental disability," which implies a condition that developed before the person was age twenty-one and that is considered to be permanent and a substantial impediment to normal functioning.[2]

Life with Chris has not always been easy. We have shared many years of struggle. At school, camp, and summer activities, Chris was always a model child. At home, however, it was a different story, and it took years of persistence, patience, and sometimes sheer grit to achieve a harmonious life with him. He learned, and I learned. I have a number of diplomas hanging on my office wall, but my most valuable degree is my M.A.M.A.—mama. All four boys have helped me matriculate toward that degree, but Chris was the major professor.

It was through Chris that I learned I also had a disability of sorts. I was unable to function well, to cope. And it was that inability to deal with my frustrations with trying to cope with Chris that led me to give up my life to Jesus Christ. With that surrender came many changes in the way I lived my life.

One of those changes was learning to discern the important from the unimportant. I have borrowed a philosophy from Dr. Robert Eliot: Rule One—Don't sweat the small stuff. Rule Two—It's all small stuff.[3] Another change was that everything took on a new perspective. It was as if I had colored lenses in my glasses instead of clear ones, and I saw the world with a different tint. I could no longer get hung up over kids that didn't use the potty on schedule, for example. Big deal. I've got a kid who is *years* behind schedule. Often that tinted perspective was what kept me sane in what often felt like an incredulously insane situation.

I have learned to see the miraculous hand of God in my life, in both the big things and the small. In 1989, my marriage of twenty-five years fell apart. The separation and subsequent divorce brought new stresses and uncertainties. However, I felt God's presence in my life in a more real and intense way than I had previously experienced. When I had to sell our house, I didn't have to put it on the market; God literally delivered buyers to my door. I believe God led me to the next place to live, when I had only thirty days to be out of the house and had no leads. I even rejoiced the day that the worker at the toll booth picked up a dime from the road and put it in the booth for me; I was out of change and didn't know how to get through the booth without incurring a fine. I see miracles when Chris finally learns, after three months of work, how to button the front of his pajamas or when a friend takes on a project to teach him to tie his shoes. I claim miracles in all sizes, shapes, and colors.

Miracles seem to abound in my world because I take nothing for granted. I have learned to drink deeply of the moments of life—to savor a balmy breeze as I walk along a beach; to marvel at the accuracy of gulls as they dive into the ocean, quickly emerge with their quarry, and do it in one seemingly effortless motion; to be in awe at the sunset of blues, oranges, and golds of the Master Painter.

I have also learned that I can look foolish and survive, that my pride is inconsequential compared to what really matters in life. Chris has given me many opportunities to learn lessons in humility. For instance, when I took Chris to a church recently, he wanted to sit in the very last row. As I started to proceed to a row in the middle of the church, Chris declared his intentions—loudly—with a four-letter word. I kept walking, pretending I hadn't heard him, wishing that a large hole would open up with a door to an underground tunnel leading to the parking lot so I could get in my car and speed away. It didn't, and we sat down and enjoyed the service, from the middle of the church. I survived. The sun came up the next day, and our names were not in the morning paper. Situations like this taught me to have a sense of humor.

In a way this book is a miracle. The idea for my first book, *Counseling Families of Children with Disabilities* (Word), came during the first International Christian Counseling Congress in Atlanta in 1988.[4] I naïvely approached the sales representative of the publisher and stated that I would like to write a book about people with disabilities for the Resources for Christian Counseling series. The discussion with that representative eventually led to a published book and then to the writing of this one.

The miracle is that my purpose in going to graduate school was to help parents of children with disabilities. I had been so frustrated by the roadblocks I encountered in finding services for Chris that I wanted to share my experiences and help others over the rough spots. When I approached Word publishers, I had no idea of the impressive credentials of the other authors in the Resources for Christian Counseling series; if I had known, I may never have been bold enough to submit a proposal. God knew all along of the best way for me to fulfill my dream. Divine vision is so much sharper and comprehensive than human vision.

As you read this book, I hope you feel that you and I are sharing our stories over a cup of coffee or tea. Writing this book gives me the opportunity to journey with you, and it is humbling for me to think of doing so. Remember as you read that you are the expert on your own child, and your story is unique and precious. Not all strategies in this book will work for you. Use what is valuable and discard the rest.

Remember that the Creator is the expert on us all. We are finite parents with limits, but he is the Limitless One who knows and loves us and our children, outrageously, without boundaries, beyond our wildest imaginings.

PART I

BEGINNING IS THE TOUGH PART

1

THE ROADS TO DIAGNOSIS

Virginia Beach, Virginia, my home, usually has unpredictable weather in February and March. One spring we experienced what seemed like all four seasons in six weeks: snow storms, a blizzard, an ice storm, snow granules, summer thundershowers, cold crisp days, balmy breezes, and several short periods of 70° and 80° temperatures.

As I was sitting on my front porch two Sundays before Easter that weird spring, enjoying the sunshine of a true spring day, I noticed a daffodil blooming beside the front step. Because some of the warm days had come early, the flowers had bloomed but then had frozen in the snow and cold weather. This daffodil somehow had come through all of that and was facing the world again.

As I looked at the daffodil, I thought of people with disabilities. This flower was no prize winner; it had damaged petals, and it didn't even stand up on its own. It leaned over to one side and might have lain on the ground if the neighboring shrub hadn't supported it. It was a faded yellow, not bright, and its petals were tinged with brown, attesting to its harsh treatment by nature. Yet it was giving life its best shot. It was responding to the sun's warmth the best way it could. It was bringing pleasure to me just by being a daffodil—by being, if you will, the very essence of daffodil-liness.

Children with disabilities and their parents are also survivors. They have much in common with the daffodil that faced an unexpected mixing of seasons. Life seems to take whimsical twists and turns, and the only thing that is certain is that nothing is certain.

The story of the three years before Chris was diagnosed is unique to our family. We had some special circumstances—the military, travel, and the Vietnam War. But I know that many threads in our story are common to all families—the uncertainties, worries, doubts, fears, as well as joys.

THE BEGINNING OF SURPRISES

As I look back on twenty-five years of our son Chris's life, I realize that most of that time was characterized by uncertainties. The discovery of pregnancy was a shock, since Jimmy, our older son, was not even six months old at the time, and another baby was the last thing I wanted. My husband, Jim, was preparing to go on a six-month Navy cruise to the Mediterranean, and I was making plans to leave Jimmy with grandparents for a few months and follow the ship to European ports with other wives. Jim was adamant about my not going to Europe while I was pregnant, so we packed our belongings, and I drove north to Pittsburgh to stay with my mother for the duration of the cruise.

The only time that was free of surprises was the pregnancy itself. I was well cared for, ate nutritious food, walked daily, didn't gain excessive weight, and saw my doctors regularly. I had no problems in the pregnancy or delivery.

However, Chris's birth gave us our first surprise. He was very unusual looking. His little ears were set low on his head and were somewhat folded over. He had a lot of hair, and it grew low on his forehead. His skin was dark bluish, and his facial expression was a frown, as if he was "worried." When I obtained the birth records from the hospital some years later, everything about Chris was listed as "normal."

The next surprise came in his feeding schedule. I had nursed Jimmy and had no problems; I was expecting to do the same with Chris. Although Chris weighed less than Jimmy had at birth, Chris wasn't satisfied with an every three- or four-hour feeding schedule. When I asked the pediatrician about this problem, he said just to feed him every four hours and not to worry; the nurses told me that the little guy was fussy and asked if I would feed him on demand. I appreciated their concern, so I fed Chris every two hours. In the hospital this wasn't so bad because other people were still bathing and changing him. But when I got home and had to care for both Chris and Jimmy, life became very busy. I don't know what I would have done had I not been living at my mother's those first six weeks. I couldn't have managed alone.

I kept looking at Chris with puzzlement, knowing that something wasn't right. He kept up the every-two-hour feeding routine much longer than I thought he would. He didn't hold up his head as well as I thought he should or respond in the ways that Jimmy had by one month of age. When I took Chris to the pediatrician for his six-week checkup, he passed muster, and the doctor never mentioned anything about possible problems.

21

MOVING AND TRAVELING TURMOIL

When Jim arrived home from his cruise, his commanding officer called and told him to report to San Diego to join a squadron that would be deploying in a few months for the western Pacific—the Vietnam War was in full swing. So we packed up and headed west by car, with two babies, ages three months and almost eighteen months.

I don't remember if I even discussed my concerns about Chris with Jim. So much was going on that it was all a blur. The Navy's unwritten rule was that the good wife was to keep family life as steady as possible so that the husband could concentrate on his job. I knew that Jim was going to war, and I wanted to be as good a wife as I could.

That was probably the worst trip of my life. Chris was fussy the entire five days. It seemed that I would just get him settled to sleep and it would be time to stop for gas. Every time we stopped, Chris would awaken and start crying again. It didn't help that my husband's agenda included making five hundred miles a day. We stopped talking to each other around Indianapolis and didn't say much until we got to San Diego and had to find an apartment.

I include this story because it's an illustration of how pressures mount. We were being uprooted and sent off to a strange place. We had to face the possibilities that could result from war. I had to think about living in a town where I knew no one and coping—alone—with two small children.

I think the reason I didn't talk with Jim about my concern for Chris was one of pure survival. It was one more stressor that just might have driven me beyond the edge of sanity at the time. My denial was a survival mechanism, because to face reality was more than I could bear at the time.

A TIME OF UNCERTAINTY

We moved into an apartment in San Diego, and then the ship left. I will never forget that day because the car battery chose to die in the first few hours I was alone. Cars seem to know when ships leave—ask any Navy wife.

I settled into a routine of caring for the children from six o'clock in the morning until seven o'clock at night, when I would collapse into bed. I took lots of pictures to send to Jim so that he could track the boys' growth while he was away. I had carefully kept a baby book about Jimmy's first few years. He was a delightful little boy and was progressing nicely. I could always find something to brag about. That first year is so special. A helpless infant becomes a walking, talking little person, and Jimmy was no exception.

Chris, however, was a different story. I didn't make many entries in his baby book—not because he was the second child and I didn't have time to do it, but because there was little to record. He just didn't seem to be making progress as fast. I remember that I would sit him up in his high chair, shove pillows in to keep him upright, and then record in the book, "sitting up today." Wishful thinking, because when I would put him on the sofa, he would tilt and slide to a lying position.

My denial was in full swing. I knew at what age Chris was supposed to sit up, and I was doing all I could to see that the reality conformed to the guidelines. The entries in the baby book reflect this ambiguity. I wrote very sketchy monthly summaries of what Chris had accomplished, and they vaguely allude to the "firsts," but I noticed a pattern of repeating those firsts. I would write one month, "a small smile now and then," and then the next month "really big smile at brother." It was a nebulous documentary of actions, without clear markers.

One of my hopes had been that because the boys were so close in age, they would become close buddies. I visualized them going off to play together and always being there for each other. This dream began to die when I realized that Chris wasn't progressing as he should and that the gap between him and Jimmy was widening.

In San Diego the boys had their normal share of colds and received routine inoculations, so they saw pediatricians periodically. At seven months of age Chris became very ill. He wouldn't eat or drink anything, and he continued to run a high fever despite antibiotics. The doctor at the Miramar Air Station clinic sent us to Balboa Naval Hospital, where Chris had a spinal tap for meningitis. The tap proved negative, and the diagnosis was of a severe ear infection that required stronger antibiotics. Again, none of the doctors noticed, or if they noticed didn't mention, that Chris was anything but a normal baby.

Chris recovered, but I was so fuzzy on his development that I wondered for many years if that infection and fever had anything to do with his disability. I've never been able to obtain an answer or investigate further because all his early medical records were later lost.

SHORE DUTY AND MORE DENIAL

Jim's ship returned after seven months, and we again had orders, this time to Pensacola, Florida. We made another cross-country drive, but I insisted that our maximum mileage was whatever we could cover in five or six hours a day. We had a pleasant trip, with time to rest and swim in the afternoons. The babies were better behaved, and Jim and I conversed the entire trip.

When we arrived in Pensacola, we bought a home within a

few days and began to live a somewhat normal existence called shore duty. There would be no deployments. Except for duty, Jim would be home every night. It was almost as if we were normal civilians. We had a house, a lawn, and a commute from the suburbs.

What wasn't normal was Chris. He didn't begin walking until he was twenty-two months old. He drooled excessively. He never made attempts to feed himself, not even to pick up the Cheerios I put on his high-chair tray. He didn't tear into the kitchen cupboards or empty out the toy box as Jimmy had done at Chris's age. He was still not sleeping through the night. When we put him into his crib, he would bang his head on the crib bars; he had a little bald spot on his forehead where he rubbed his head. He would play with one toy in one way for months on end.

Jim and I would look at him and say that we either had a very serious problem or an eccentric genius on our hands. Neither one of us was willing to pursue the reality that there was a problem; all we did was look and wonder.

It didn't occur to us that we were ignoring the obvious. Even when one of our neighbors, who had a deaf son, told us how she had denied her son's deafness until he was over a year old, I didn't realize that I was in denial.

Unfortunately, our shore duty wasn't a happy time in our marriage. I didn't know until many years later that my husband came back from the Vietnam air war with a lot of unresolved issues. He never discussed them with me; I'm not sure that he was aware of them himself. We didn't have emotional intimacy, and being together every day only served to focus a bright light on how empty our relationship had become.

I don't remember what finally propelled me to face facts, but I finally made a doctor's appointment to discuss Chris's delays in development. "Don't worry," I was told. "You are just an overly concerned mother. He'll come along just like your other son." I wasn't satisfied to hear this, so I made another appointment with the senior pediatrician on staff at the hospital. He ordered X rays of Chris's ankles and wrists. I remembered from college that these were sometimes used as indicators of development. When I returned the next week to hear the results, the doctor said that everything was normal. When I pressed for more details, he repeated himself and said he had nothing more to say—and left.

I have asked myself hundreds of times why I accepted that opinion and didn't go further to get some answers. Guilt haunted me about what I should have done better. If I had pursued the issue, I used to think, perhaps Chris would have been in a preschool program earlier and would have received crucial early intervention, avoiding some of his developmental delays. For many years I took on all of the blame—and all of the worry—for Chris. I still have to fight these tendencies; I don't know if they'll ever leave completely.

It's hard to look back and recall motives for actions. I can only recall circumstances, and when I do, it makes perfect sense that I stopped looking for an answer at that point. I was only twenty-five years old and was living far away from where I had been raised. I didn't know any civilian doctors; I trusted the Navy doctors and wasn't given any referrals. I was probably hoping against hope that they were right about Chris's normality and held on to that slim thread.

Other factors were also at play. I mentioned that our marriage wasn't going well, so this wasn't "our" issue as much as it was mine. Family had a part also, as none of my "elders," those parents and aunts and uncles who were part of my guidance system while growing up, ever indicated that they had any concerns about Chris. Later, one person indicated that she "always knew there was something wrong," but either I didn't hear or the words were never spoken aloud to me. I suspect the latter.

I've often wondered what dynamics were operating in this conspiracy of silence. Did my family just think it was not polite to discuss this? Did they want to talk but just didn't know the right words? Were they aware but ashamed or embarrassed? In the late sixties, children with disabilities were often still shunted away or kept hidden; the only adults with disabilities I knew were the beggars on the city streets and one church member who had to wear a special shoe because one leg was shorter than the other.

I didn't ever see babies or little children with disabilities. I had visited some special schools as part of my course work in college, but that was very limited exposure. One family friend had an older Down Syndrome boy whom we would occasionally visit, but he lived away at school. Our family had a distant cousin with a mentally disabled older daughter; they viewed her with pity and spoke of her as "funny." How could I begin to approach anyone in that generation with my own fears?

It also didn't help that life in suburban Pensacola was expensive. Purchasing a home, a car, and some unwise investments were more than we could handle. After one year we sold our house and moved into base housing. Quarters were new, very nice, and certainly more convenient for Jim's work. The moving, however, occupied time and effort and provided a diversion from concerns about Chris—and our own problems.

Little hassles began to pile up and affect daily life. Chris couldn't go out and play with the other children as his brother did. I had a toddler-sized baby on my hands. We used the base nursery for baby-sitting service occasionally. I remember practically begging the staff to allow Chris to take a nap and

27

use a crib, even though he was past their two-year-old limit for these activities. I stopped placing him in the nursery because I felt he wasn't safe with the other children his age. Using the nursery at church was another struggle; Chris required special instructions, and I had to keep praying for understanding baby-sitters.

ANOTHER MOVE AND A DIAGNOSIS

We were scheduled to be on shore duty three years, but Jim was unhappy in his staff/teaching assignment and wanted to return to flying. He applied for, and received, orders back to a flying squadron with sea duty.

In this move we literally traveled into a diagnosis, without actively pursuing one. I have often wondered if that was divine intervention—God propelling us when we were too frozen to move on our own. Jim was required to spend a few months in the training squadron in Key West before reporting to his squadron in Virginia Beach. We decided that I would spend that time in Pittsburgh. The children and I could live on the third floor of my mother's house, and I could do substitute teaching a few days a week. Both grandmas had agreed to take turns baby-sitting when I needed them. Jim and I had decided we would set up housekeeping in Virginia when he joined the command. When I reflect on those days, I think we should have had a Gypsy wagon instead of a car—it would have been more appropriate.

We had the movers pack our belongings and ship them to storage in Virginia Beach. We stuffed the car with what I would need for a few months for the kids and drove to Pittsburgh.

At this point Providence took over. Chris had developed an

infection on his knee during the two-day trip. When we arrived in Pittsburgh, we took him to an emergency room, and the doctor on duty said it must have been an insect bite and gave us some topical medication. The next few days Chris's knee looked worse, so I made an appointment with a female pediatrician whom I didn't know. I had always been intrigued when I passed her office—a home in a beautiful park-like setting, and on that basis alone I made the appointment.

Chris's knee infection was impetigo. But that wasn't the real news. The pediatrician said that although it was difficult for her to tell us, she felt that our three-year-old was behaving more like an eighteen-month-old child and that we should have some psychological evaluations done. We took Chris to Children's Hospital for testing. It was there that we first heard the word "retarded." The psychologist with whom we had a very brief interview told us in a matter-of-fact manner that Chris was severely retarded and that we needed to think about what we wanted to do. We set an appointment for me to return.

THE BEGINNINGS OF REALITY

I never kept that appointment. Jim had arrived in Virginia Beach for his first set of schools and decided that he was lonely. He called and said he had rented a house and was coming to Pittsburgh to get us. I have no idea now, years later, why I agreed to move again, so soon after just getting settled and knowing that I would be spending time in Virginia Beach without him. Perhaps I was young enough to be persuaded by his loneliness, but that's just a guess.

The result of the decision was that I was back in Virginia Beach. I knew the town's physical layout, but I had no knowledge of its available services. For the first time I had a name for my son's problem, so armed with that, I began making phone calls. Eventually one call led to another, and I found some help.

Chris was re-examined, and we received more information, some of it helpful and some not. We learned through genetic testing that Chris didn't have Down Syndrome. That news came right on the heels of another discovery—that I was again pregnant. We breathed a long sigh of relief to know that one possibility had been ruled out; but we were still left with a lot of questions, and another baby on the way.

The second part of the diagnosis was useless. The doctor confirmed that Chris was indeed mentally retarded. He advised us to place Chris in a residential home, which, he added, many prominent citizens of the area had done in similar circumstances. We should concentrate on raising our older child and forget about Chris because he would never progress beyond the level of a five- or six-year-old. I remember becoming extremely angry and telling the doctor that he had no right to make such a prediction about a child who was only three years old. I stormed out of his office and never spoke with him again.

That is the story of our trail to diagnosis. We were left with a generic description, a dismal prediction, and disastrous advice. The only positive aspect of this time of our lives was that, for some unknown reason, Jim and I both had an inner peace about the coming baby.

FEELINGS

However, my feelings about Chris were a jumble. Caring for him was exhausting. Chris had some unique characteristics, among them the knack of being extremely well behaved in school settings but very resistant at home. He resisted any change, such as getting in and out of cars, out of a tub, and into and out of clothing. It was hard work, and as my pregnancy progressed, I became more and more exhausted.

During the three years that we looked for a diagnosis, many feelings emerged. I felt lonely, isolated, and alienated. Part of this was because of the lack of intimacy in our marriage as well as Jim's deployments, but part was also because it became quickly apparent that our family didn't fit in with other families. It was a great effort to arrange for a day at the park or the beach with others. Chris required so much attention that he consumed my energy. I couldn't predict his behavior as I could my first child's, and I never knew what might make him unhappy and fussy.

I also kept busy, probably so that I wouldn't have to pay attention to the nagging doubts I carried in my heart. My active denial system was fed with an element of false hope. Perhaps our observations were wrong, and things would be all right after all. Perhaps something miraculous would occur, and Chris would catch up. I was a churchgoer at the time, and I believed in God, but I hadn't developed any kind of personal relationship with the Lord. I never thought of praying. My hope was more on the order of a wish.

I kept trying to maintain the appearance of normalcy. I kept a very tidy and nicely decorated house. I was active in the Officers' Wives' club. I sewed clothing and did crafts. I did volunteer work, even taking on the integration of a segregated public-school class for black children with disabilities. I kept moving, because to keep moving meant I wasn't dying, at least physically.

The crisis of Chris's diagnosis wasn't an event that happened in isolation. Our family may have had more dramatic circumstances than most—another pregnancy, several moves, father gone several times for long periods—but each family has its own circumstances. Also, the diagnosis at age three was only the first diagnosis. It's common for families to pass this crisis several times. It's also common *not* to have an accurate diagnosis.

You may sense your child has a developmental delay of some kind, but you may not know a name for that delay for several years. Medical knowledge and technology have progressed substantially in the past twenty years. Chris was eighteen when we received a diagnosis of a genetic disorder, and even that is at ninety-five-percent probability. We still have questions because we have no family history of the disorder, and we therefore have to assume that it is a mutation. If Chris's condition is what we were told, Coffin-Lawry Syndrome, then it can only be transmitted by Chris himself or through a female, and I have no female children. However, the small nagging question remains—what if the five-percent margin of error is that—the error. What about our other sons and their future children? The odds are in their favor, but their experience makes them more aware of the possibility of problems.

I recently read of a mother who spent five years in obtaining a diagnosis for her daughter.[1] The mother knew at birth that there was something wrong, and the pediatrician told the parents at six months not to worry. At eight months they received a referral to a neurologist but had to go through two more neurologists in the next four years to have a name for their daughter's genetic disorder. This mother said she was one of the lucky parents to have a named disorder; most of the parents she met knew only that their child was delayed but the cause of the delay was "unknown origin."

Not all parents will have a specific name or cause of their child's disorder. Parents who have a child with learning disabilities know that something is not right with their baby. As the child grows into a toddler and preschooler, people describe the child as "difficult." The child has a short attention span, doesn't seem to concentrate, doesn't play well with other children in the neighborhood, seems not to be able to speak as well as other children, or sometimes doesn't seem to hear or understand what the parents say. The child may be just generally "discontented." But it's not until the child fails at academic tasks that a diagnosis of learning disabilities is discovered. Then all of the earlier problems make sense.

THOUGHTS AND NOTES FOR PARENTS

As I reflect on these early years of Chris's life, I wonder what would have been helpful for me to know. What would I have liked to see happen? What could I have done better in the circumstances? I offer the following checklist as a help to parents (or friends and relatives of parents) who may be at the stage of looking for a diagnosis.

- If you have concerns about your child, don't be afraid to discuss them with other people. If you aren't getting help from your doctor, then discuss the matter with your close friends or relatives whom you feel may be of help. Having a child with a problem isn't anything to feel ashamed of, and your friends may have been noticing specific inconsistencies with your child. You might have an opportunity to broaden your support system by opening up to others.
- Trust your own instincts and become assertive in obtaining a diagnosis if you feel that you aren't satisfied. Don't be afraid to seek out other medical opinions. Don't ignore the doubts of your own heart.
- A word of caution: When you do receive confirmed

medical information with a diagnosis, you may still want a second opinion. That's reasonable. If you find yourself jumping from doctor to doctor, trying to prove that your child doesn't have a problem or to obtain a less severe diagnosis, then check your own motives. You could be getting into a situation that will benefit neither you nor your child.

- Try to keep accurate records of your child's development and of your own daily thoughts. Your written observations of your own child are extremely valuable. Our memories are selective when we are asked to recall events, and having a written record will be a great advantage. In the record or journal, also enter a note of each doctor's visit, with names, dates, procedures, and comments.

- Ask for specific information about examinations and tests; record the information you are given. It's too easy to become intimidated by medical personnel and then be afraid to ask questions because you don't want to be seen as stupid. When professionals use jargon (the terminology of their profession) and we aren't acquainted with the terms, we may hesitate to ask questions because we don't know the proper use or pronunciation of those terms. Never forget that you are the consumer of medical services and you have a right to ask any questions you may have. Insist that medical terminology be explained to you in words that you can understand.

- Ask your doctor for copies of articles that explain your child's condition or for names and sources of books that would be useful. If your doctor doesn't have this information, then ask him or her to obtain it for you. If you live in a large city with a medical school, you could

ask for information on how to research the topic
yourself.

- Look for resources that will help you take care of
yourself during this difficult time. No matter how severe
the problems you are having because of your child, you
still must care for yourself in order to be able to help
your child. You need rest, recreation, prayer, and
nutrition. You may have other children who need your
care. You may need to enlist some help with childcare or
housekeeping. If both parents work, you may need to
reassess delegation of chores. If you are a single parent,
you may need to prioritize what you are doing and
decide how you can build in supports for yourself.
- A note to friends and relatives: Be honest and express
concerns openly. It didn't help me to hear "I told you so"
remarks years later. It only added to my guilt. You need
to be gentle when you help parents deal with reality. Try
to gather some concrete information that the parents can
use. A group, personal contact, book, clinic—any of
these could lead to more information for a parent.

Dealing with a diagnosis of a disability requires tremendous emotional energy. Parents need to do all that they can to
take care of themselves, become informed, and care for the
child. Whether the diagnosis is received before the child is
born, at the time of the birth, or several months or years later,
the dynamics remain the same.

2

TELLING YOUR STORY

Once you receive a diagnosis about your child, you will be telling the child's story for years to come. Announcements, so to speak, will be made to friends and relatives about the nature of the disability. The story will be told to professionals to whom you go for services—medical, social, and educational. You will have to "explain" the child to people involved in some way with care—the nursery workers at church, baby-sitters, the person who cuts the child's hair, the dentist, the teacher, the school-bus driver. This is only a partial list of people who will require information to be of assistance and support to the child.

You will also find yourselves telling the child's story to a wider range of people. The litany above involves those who have a "need to know." Many more people, who aren't connected by relationship or by the services they provide, will hear your child's story. These people are curious about the child and in most cases are sincerely interested and not being nosey or rude. I suggest that you rehearse and perfect a story for such cases and give pertinent information without allowing it to be invasive.

You'll find that your story changes as your own understanding and experiences change. You must analyze what you are saying to yourselves and to each other. This self-examination will occur at several points in your life. It's as if your life is a play, with the curtain slowly parting from the center, each time revealing more insight into your situation.

ACTION, NOT REACTION

To look retrospectively on my past actions and discover motivations is relatively easy. Hindsight is twenty-twenty, the old saying goes. It takes far more energy to look into where I am now and what is guiding my present activity. I have acquired this skill over many years and with much practice. If I had had this ability when my children were younger, I probably could have *acted* purposefully rather than *reacted* to my situation.

The "action-not-reaction" concept can be especially crucial when the discovery/diagnosis is relatively new. Being able to act rather than react allows you to explore options at varying points in the child's life when decisions must be made regarding schooling or care.

DEALING WITH ANGER

The first step for parents is to be aware of your own feelings when you learn of your child's disability. With awareness comes acknowledgment, then permission to experience those feelings. Problems arise when you deny feelings of anger or despair.

Anger is a particular problem. Many of us have been taught that "negative" feelings aren't nice, especially for Christians. You are told that if you are feeling angry, then there must be something wrong. But anger can be legitimate. Christ's anger at the moneychangers in the Temple is an example of justifiable anger. When anger is the result of specific causes for specific, unrighteous consequences, then the anger is both lawful and focused.

However, when you feel anger because of your child's disability, the issue is much more complex. In most cases, the cause of a child's disability is unknown, and parental anger is undifferentiated. This type of anger is uncomfortable. Everything and everyone—including yourself—are potential targets of this type of anger. The result is a vague, constant dissatisfaction and anxiety about life. To relieve those unpleasant feelings, the anger seeks a target.

You may feel anger at the child but then reason it away, knowing that the child hasn't done anything to deserve the anger except exist, and even that wasn't the child's choice, it was yours. You may then reject the child as a target of anger because it seems illogical and is therefore unacceptable. In addition, you may feel very ill at ease with conscious rejection of your own child and will not allow yourself to experience feelings of anger toward the child. In some cases, however, you may become so overwhelmed by anger that the child becomes a scapegoat for all that is wrong in your life. Child abuse is much higher in families with disabled children; the additional stress of caring for this child, added to other stressors in life, becomes too much for parents to bear.

You may find you direct your anger toward a specific doctor or hospital. Unless you can point to a clear case of negligence or medical malpractice, you have no reason for being angry with the doctor. However, the desire to lay blame for an unpleasant event is very strong. One of the most logical places to lay that blame is on the ones to whom you've entrusted your child's care. The fact that the doctor had nothing to do with the child's disability doesn't protect him or her from your anger; you may think that doctors should have done something else. This anger may also carry over to all medical personnel and affect your dealings with them.

You may decide to be angry at yourself for being the cause of your child's disability. Even if you never committed any intentional harmful actions, the mere fact that you donated an egg or sperm that could carry a defect is enough cause for you to be angry at yourself. Anger at self is safer than anger at others. Somehow, in our Christian world, this is allowable, even though it isn't healthy.

Most Christians don't allow themselves the luxury of expressing or even feeling anger at God. Because feeling anger at God is such a strong taboo, people turn that anger in on themselves. The following line of reasoning may prevail: If I believe in a God and call myself Christian, if I have lived by the rules of the Bible, if I have been faithful in attendance and service to my church, then how could God have permitted this to happen? There must be some master plan that includes this punishment. It isn't fair. God is out to get me (or us). In other words, God is powerful, and I am powerless. I am a puppet in God's hands, and this child is one more reminder of how helpless I am in the face of a controlling God. Since God is always good, I must be bad.

Several irrational lines of thought are possible from applying this logic. The following chart lists some irrational thoughts that parents of a child with a disability may have and the rational, healthy thoughts that can replace them.

IRRATIONAL THOUGHTS	RATIONAL THOUGHTS
I (we) must have done something to deserve this.	No one did anything. This is something that just happened.
God saw that things were going too well for me (us), so he sent this.	God doesn't inflict harm on innocent children to punish adults.
The child's problems exist so God can perform a miracle and bring others to salvation.	Miracles are always possible, but we can't claim to know the mind of God.
If I (we) devote my life to this child, I will show others what a good and deserving person I am.	My worth in Christ doesn't depend on what I do. If I make mistakes, I'm still okay with God.
Having this child will not change anything in our family. We will have a totally normal life.	We will have to adapt and adjust. Things will be very different from what we expected them to be.
We can't let others know that we don't always feel okay.	It's okay to be human and to let others know that we are.
I (we) can't bear this burden.	I can't bear this alone, but with God, all things are possible.
It is always an uphill fight; everyone is against me (us).	Not everyone is an enemy. I will find people who can be of support in my life.
So and so is to blame for all of this.	Trying to find and place blame can take a lot of my time and energy and may impede my relationships to others.

You can take steps to deal with your anger. The first step is to recognize that undifferentiated anger comes from unmet expectations. When my children don't do chores that I have expected them to do, I become angry. When a friend treats me in an unpleasant and unexpected way, I feel anger. When life doesn't turn out the way you thought it should, you feel anger. In a way, saying that life doesn't treat you as you had anticipated is saying that God doesn't treat you as you assumed he would.

The second step is to change your expectations. I have learned to remind myself that this life is only temporal. We all know that, but somehow we have to go back to this basic principle occasionally. I find that Romans 8:28 is a great comfort to me: "And we know that in all things God works for the good of those who love him, who have been called according to his purpose." God is in control, working for my family's good. Another passage that provides consolation is Revelation 7:15–17, which describes heaven and concludes: "God will wipe away every tear from their eyes."

I know that in eternity I will experience Chris as whole and complete, that his body will be like the body of the risen Lord, without any flaws. We will spend eternity without tears, praising God, in joy.

I didn't automatically come to the point of using these Scripture passages and thoughts to guide my life. But once I did learn them, I found that focusing on these principles has kept me focused on God and not myself. My expectations have indeed changed. It's not my will, but his. And I trust that his will is for Chris's good.

When I do feel anger, and I occasionally do, I examine it closely. If I'm angry because of a particular situation, I look to see how I can be part of the solution, not just stew about the problem. I may have to alter my expectations or false beliefs. I may have to let go of something and just trust God to work it out. Each situation is different. The critical factor is that I don't become immobilized by the anger, that it doesn't control me. Paradoxically, putting God in control allows me to have more control over areas of my life because I can move in peace. My decisions aren't clouded over by destructive emotions that are keeping me from a full experience of God's love and provision. I can recognize anger for what it is—a temporary feeling that I can divert and control.

TELLING THE STORY TO YOURSELF AND EACH OTHER

How you deal with your anger will drive what you tell yourself and your spouse about this child. It may even be a central component in whether or not you are able to communicate your feelings honestly about the child with each other. You must learn how to tell each other about your fears and doubts as well as your hopes and dreams. You also need to listen to each other and accept the other's feelings. If you haven't dealt with your own feelings candidly, you will feel uncomfortable with the other's feelings. For example, a father not comfortable with his own fear for his child's future will not be able to tolerate his spouse's uncertainties. He will want her to have some answers to calm his own fears, and if the solutions aren't forthcoming, he can't accept her fear because it raises his own anxiety.

You must be open with each other in what you tell each other about this child. If not, you will end up playing games and will set up a pattern of interaction that will only trap both of you in an elaborate web before you know what has happened to you. One spouse may try to soften life for the other and not discuss feelings. This may take the form of thinking, "He [or she] has enough stress at work, and I shouldn't burden him [or her] with this."

One parent may reject the child, feeling that the disability is a direct reminder of an inability to produce a perfect offspring. The other parent may overcompensate to try to get the rejecting parent to accept the child. He or she may buy expensive clothing to make the child look as cute as possible. A mother or father may make the child the focus of family attention as much as possible so that the other will accept the child. The parents may think that if they just don't discuss their feelings that the pain will go away and all will be well.

TELLING THE CHILDREN

Ultimately, what you tell yourselves and each other will affect all of your other "tellings"—to your other children, to family, to friends, to strangers. An extension of the telling is the interacting. We communicate in two ways, verbal and nonverbal. Both are controlled by our beliefs—what we have told ourselves. We communicate far more by our nonverbal actions than by our words. Our words may be very carefully chosen to convey one message, but our body language, expression, and tone of voice convey another. Our actions do indeed speak louder than our words. Children are very perceptive in figuring out what we are really all about. Children acquire information on several levels.

When you wonder how best to explain verbally the developmental delays in a child to your other children, remember this: Teaching children about their brother or sister with a disability isn't much different from teaching them about other things in life—how to handle money, who God is, or what sex is all about. You give the information that is appropriate for their age, developmental level, and curiosity. Use words that are appropriate to their understanding and deal in reality, without sugarcoating the issue or being overly pessimistic.

I remember how ten-year-old Shawn, our youngest son, who learned German in fourth grade, still couldn't quite understand why Chris, then eighteen, couldn't be told once to do something and immediately understand. "But Mom," Shawn said, "why can't he just think about it?" Shawn knew that his brother was in special education, was slower or sometimes unable to grasp rules of games, and still needed help with many things, but he couldn't compute why Chris couldn't think things through as he could. I've had to review the story of Chris's disability to each of the children many times, over their many ages.

As our family changes, I find myself repeating a different story. Right now the story includes Chris's current living situation and projections for his future. As our sons grow older, they are becoming more interested in their part in Chris's future. Again, they seem to absorb bits and pieces of the story as their interests and maturity levels change. They are beginning to recognize the interrelatedness of all of our lives, particularly that we will all be actively involved with Chris in some way as long as he and we are alive.

You also tell your child's story in nonverbal ways—in how you interact with the child with the disability. Children will observe whether you or your spouse or both are feeding, changing, bathing, holding, and rocking the baby. They will note your tone of voice when you deal with this child. They will listen as you talk to each other about the child. They will pick up fragments of your conversations with others—in person or over the phone—even though they may appear to have no interest at all in your conversation.

The intensity of your distress over the situation of the child with the disability will also be conveyed to your children, both in words and actions. Even though they may be too young to understand the actual content of your conversations, they will know from your nonverbal signals if you are happy and peaceful or fretful and tense.

Any of several possible events can cause you stress. Your disabled child could be in a life-threatening situation. The child could be medically stable but require intense care at home. You may be frustrated with not knowing what is wrong and may be searching for help and resources. Any of these situations can drain your limited emotional energy, time, and finances. You have only so much to give out in a twenty-four-hour day. You need a certain amount of rest and nourishment. Your mind needs time to process and sort. Your bank accounts have clear limits.

When your family has a child with a disability, it's almost as if you are on an amusement park ride. When you step into the car of a roller coaster, someone else holds the controls. There are no stops or stations along the way. You are committed to be in that car until the end of the ride. The care of your child will be a constant in your life; you're on the ride until it stops. You won't have the luxury of stopping the ride for a rest. You will have family business, other children, and other stresses to cope with in addition to the child with special needs.

Modeling provides a powerful learning experience. Your children will do as you do, not as you say. If there is a discrepancy between your words and your actions, your children will choose to imitate your actions. Actions result from attitudes, so in imitating parental actions, children incorporate parental attitudes without conscious awareness. The messages, then, that you send to your other children are the messages that you tell yourself and each other.

The best situation is that the parents have a solid marriage coupled with a strong faith. They feel secure in themselves and in their relationship to each other. The content of what they say to themselves and to each other reflects an attitude of trust in each other and trust in God to work this situation through, even though they may not be certain of the outcome. They are aware that life is changing, that the problems with this child were unexpected, but that God will provide what they need in terms of time, energy, and other resources to care for their entire family and each other.

This, of course, is the ideal. Real life occurs on a continuum somewhere between the stargazing ideal and cynical despair, fluctuating between several levels. You may be totally unaware of what you are modeling; however, your children are observing, absorbing, and learning as they watch you play out the family drama.

TELLING RELATIVES

Life doesn't happen in nice, neat compartments. We rarely have the luxury of dealing with only one component of a crisis at a time. In fact, the constitution of a crisis is such that many things happen at once, and we become stressed out because we can't bear it all. We usually don't have the luxury of dealing with the news of our child's disability sequentially—first as individuals, then as a couple, next with our children, and then with extended family and the rest of the world.

Often it all happens at once. When we get the news, we have to share it with others. What's more, we may be telling others before we have an opportunity to sort through our own feelings. It's more likely that we are still in the midst of emotional turmoil ourselves while being faced with others who are also feeling confusion and pain.

Telling others about the child brings reactions, and those reactions can cause problems. It would be nice if relatives had a red warning button that would flash when they were about to say something detrimental to the mental health of the parents. People don't intend meanness, but comments often are hurtful. Denial from others is particularly painful. "He'll grow out of it," is a statement that I remember hearing after telling a friend of Chris's diagnosis. The unspoken comment that I inferred was, "I can't handle hearing this from you, and I don't want to discuss it. I'm very uncomfortable, and I don't know what to say, so let's say nothing. All I want to hear from you is good news about Chris, so talk about him when you have some."

Another comment was, "We won't use the word 'mentally retarded'; he's just slow, and that's what we'll tell others." When someone very close to me said this, I was crushed. I felt as if that person was ashamed of me for producing this defective child and that I was bringing shame to others. I felt as if I was suddenly someone to be pitied.

Another reaction is the one I call the "Spanish Inquisition." You are given a series of questions, such as "Did you do anything in your pregnancy? Did anything happen at birth? Was it the doctor's fault? Why didn't you do anything sooner?" When their questions are answered, these people give you nothing back, but nod their head, satisfied that they have done what they are supposed to do, and walk away.

As I mentioned earlier, one of the most difficult statements that I had to handle was someone telling me a few years ago, "I always knew there was something wrong with that baby." What amazed me about this statement is that when Chris was a baby, this person never uttered a word about having suspicions to me. The "I knew it all along" statement is of no value; it left me wanting to *scream*, "Where were you with all of your wisdom when I needed your support?"

Parents, particularly mothers, need to protect themselves

from others. One way to do this is to maintain a good offense.
There are several ways to do this.

Think about yourself first. You aren't responsible for everyone else's emotions or reactions, beyond your other children.
All of these other people are adults and are accountable for
their own feelings. It's *not* your job to protect them from real
life.

Be honest to others about how you are feeling. You aren't
obliged to keep up a good front to make anyone else feel
better.

*Tell what you know about your child simply and with whatever
facts you may have.* If the story has missing pieces, just say that.
Indicate that there is still a lot you don't know.

Don't allow blaming. You may have to risk offending
someone by saying, "You may think [I did something wrong
during the pregnancy or the doctor is at fault or this is a
punishment for sin], but that's not the case. If you keep
talking in this manner, then I can't talk with you any longer."

Don't accept advice unless it makes sense to you. Listen to
everything, but evaluate. You might get tired of hearing,
"You should . . ." or "If I were you, I would. . . ." You can
pleasantly say, "I appreciate your concern. We will think over
what you've said." You are under no obligation to do what
anyone says. This is your child, and you must do what you
think is best. If well-meaning relatives ask you why you didn't
follow their advice, you can tell them that it just didn't work
out. You may have to become more assertive and tell them
that while you know that they mean well, this is none of their

business. When you have a baby, suddenly everyone around you becomes a child-rearing expert. When you have a child with a problem, these experts often want to "fix" the problem for you—to make them feel better.

Accept help and support that is offered. Sometimes we want to remain fiercely independent. I noticed this trait in myself when I was younger and felt less secure in my role as a mother. I almost resented what I interpreted to be interference in my parenting and worked hard to establish that I was a competent mother who could make satisfactory rules for her children. I let go of that eventually and allowed more direct help. Allow others to rock a fussy baby to sleep or to take a child for a walk so you can get some rest. If someone asks, "What can I do?" tell exactly what you need, whether it is meal help, household help, or childcare. Occasional spoiling will not corrupt a baby or young child; I could let go of my rules now and then. The more children I had and the more difficult the tasks of mothering became, the more I welcomed relief.

TELLING STRANGERS

People will ask you about your child out of politeness, genuine concern, and sometimes curiosity. Often it's not apparent that a child has a disability, and little has to be said at this time. Neighbors may ask, "How's your son?" and you may choose to disclose information or simply reply with "Fine," if that's the case. If you choose to discuss your child's condition, you will find yourself dealing with a variety of reactions, just as you do with relatives and close friends. It helps to be prepared with a simple description of what is happening. You don't have to disclose details of your life to everyone who asks.

If your child has physical problems that are visible, it is less easy to avoid stares and questions of others. A nice smile back to people who stare often works well. If you have a name for the child's problem, you can also simply say, "She has cerebral palsy [or whatever your child has]." I have found that people who are interested in my child usually have children or siblings with disabilities and are truly empathic toward me. They just want to say that they have been through this too.

TELLING PROFESSIONALS

Most professionals, I believe, work with children and adults with disabilities out of genuine interest and concern. What we parents must do is recognize that these professionals are people, and they can make mistakes. Sometimes, as a parent, I feel as if it's me against "them." The truth is these are professionals with a particular expertise acting in a certain role, often bounded by institutional rules and regulations.

Maintain as much control and responsibility for your own situation as possible and learn to work within the system. Your approach should be that of a *team* working together for the child, not as opponents in a struggle. Not all professionals will be receptive to that approach, and not all encounters will yield the results that you want, but a shared-responsibility approach is more likely to be successful.

When you tell professionals about your child, keep these things in mind. They may increase your chance at success in interpersonal relationships with the professionals you encounter.

Record your observations. You may want to begin a three-ring binder with some sectional divisions. One section might be for your own notes made at home, another for questions that occur to you to ask as they arise, before the appointment. In another section keep copies of records. You are entitled to copies of reports written about your child.

Write down responses to your questions. When you are in an appointment and you don't understand something the medical person says, ask for clarification. Ask doctors to spell names of procedures or medicines. Ask about possible reactions to medicines, dosage directions, and how the medicine should be administered. If the doctor says that directions will be on the bottle, don't accept this response. Often the labels aren't as complete as they should be. Insist that your doctor gives you the information.

Ask questions about referrals. If you are given a referral, ask whether this is the only doctor available, why this particular doctor is being recommended, exactly what should you expect from that doctor, and what is to be gained from the referral.

Write out a brief history of your pregnancy, delivery, and significant events in the baby's life and keep it up-to-date. You will be asked these same questions again and again. If you have the details written out, your responses will be consistent and clear. Also, reading off information makes you look more authoritative and sure of yourself.

Being able to speak of your child with others in an assured manner conveys that you are competent and in control. It enables you to be an effective partner with others in obtaining the best services available for your child.

3

WHAT NEXT?
THE CHANGES
IN YOUR LIFE

Our family likes to do puzzles. Sometimes in the winter months we set up a puzzle on the game table in the family room. As one of us has time and interest, we sit down and work on the puzzle. We have put together puzzles of three hundred, five hundred, a thousand, and, if we were especially ambitious, fifteen hundred pieces. No matter the size of the puzzle, the result was always a completed, flat, smooth picture.

I sometimes think of life as a puzzle, except that we never have all of the pieces when we begin—we get them only one piece at a time. In cardboard puzzles, we always expect the pieces to fit in orderly fashion to produce a finished picture. When I think about our family in terms of a jigsaw puzzle, I have a slightly different image. I think of each person and event in the family as a puzzle piece that is supposed to fit together to form the whole. However, Chris is one piece that will not quite fit into a flat, smooth, completed puzzle. We want him there because the part of the picture that is printed on him completes our family scene, but somehow his "tabs" don't quite fit. To include him as he is and complete the picture means that the puzzle will always have a bump because of a forced fit. For Chris to fit, other pieces around him have to be changed and adapted, so that we can achieve as complete a picture as possible when we are all pieced together.

Of course, all families must shift and adapt as children and parents grow, develop, and change. But the family who has a child with special needs will always be faced with that child not changing, growing, and developing on the same type of timetable as the other children. The child will be the source of the bulge that can't be smoothed away in the picture.

In order to remain a healthy family, you must realize that you will *always* be required to be flexible and adaptable around the child with a disability. Change becomes the norm in life. I have found stability to be the exception rather than the rule in Chris's life. Even when he has been in residential programs, any number of things changed, and those changes affected not only him but also the rest of us. Policies, procedures, and personnel changes all occur, often without any warning. The family can't control these shifts because they occur in systems in which the family has no voice.

When Chris was seven, we placed him in the Devereaux School in West Chester, Pennsylvania. It was a difficult decision for us, but with the circumstances at the time, we felt it was the right choice. He was nearing the end of his second year there when we were informed that the tuition rates were rising dramatically, more than we could afford. Suddenly we had to change our way of life to accommodate Chris living at home again, now with three other brothers. Our family had no voice in that tuition raise. No one consulted us to find out what this change might mean to our family. And no one offered to help us explore other options. We had to cope and absorb the change immediately, on our own.

CHANGE IN THE IMPACT OF THE DIAGNOSIS

When you receive your child's diagnosis, you must deal with it at that point, but you also will continue to deal with the effect of that diagnosis over time. I believe that the initial impact does diminish over time as we become involved with all of the other issues that the initial news conveys. At some place, the influence of the diagnosis reaches a vanishing point as other tasks require attention. The name of the child's condition remains the same, but its meaning changes for us over months and years.

Medical Aspects

If your child has a physical problem or a physical problem plus a developmental delay, your family faces another layer of possible changes. The child might develop additional complications or infections. You may find you live in a constant state of vigilance. For example, if your child has a shunt (a tube that drains fluid from the brain into the stomach), you may always be watching for signs of malfunction. If that occurs, you know you face various possibilities, from correction of the problem with the shunt to the child's dying.

As your child grows older, additional problems may develop. A child with partial paralysis of the legs may begin to develop kidney problems. A Down Syndrome child may begin having heart problems. Recently, adults who had polio as children and seemed to have conquered the disease are finding that they are regressing. Many who had built productive lives are now unable to work and live life as they did before. There was no way to predict that this would occur.

Positive changes may also occur. New drugs, treatments, or programs may be available to your child, changing the original prognosis. Since most diagnoses of developmental delay are fairly vague, your child may achieve more than was ever thought possible.

Social Changes

When children are very young, a disability interferes less with play and peer interaction. The child with special needs often can fit in with younger children or enjoy parallel play. By the age of six, children are involved in more complicated play and recreational activities: scouting programs, T-ball, soccer, swimming, gymnastics, dance lessons, and flag football, to name a few. The child with a developmental delay may become isolated and lonely as former playmates enjoy team and group pursuits.

Families also often form friendships as they gather to watch their children participate in these activities over the years. Your child with a disability may not attend the events, or you and your spouse may take turns attending and lose the ability to enjoy friendships as a family with other families.

Family Role Changes

One of the dangers in a family with a disabled child is becoming cast into fixed roles. When our children were young, particularly when Jim was away on Navy travels, my role was fixed into childcare and home management. When Jim was away, I functioned as a single parent, except that I had a source of income and therefore was not responsible for providing money for us to live. That fixed role was stressful to me, and I found myself devising as many ways as I could to follow interests that would allow me to continue to grow as a person. Because I didn't have to work outside the home, I could volunteer my time to stay connected with the outside world and keep myself from suffocating in the demands of home and children.

Mothers are often the primary caregivers to the child with special needs. If a mother wants to make changes and meets resistance from her husband, a marital crisis may develop. Or parents may feel they are the only ones who can take care of the child, particularly if the child has medical problems. The parents may never be able to have time to themselves because of this imposed rule.

Sue wanted a weekend away with her husband, but Jed expressed concern about leaving their son in somebody else's care. He grudgingly gave in, saying to Sue, "You make all the arrangements, and I'll agree." After spending a great deal of time and energy writing out instructions, Sue felt resentful and guilty the entire weekend they were away because all the responsibility had been placed on her.

I didn't realize how locked into routine my life had been until Chris no longer lived at home. I'm amazed at how flexible I can now be, after almost twenty-two years of having my life ruled by his schedule. I also wasn't aware of how I had carried over this structure into all other parts of my life. Because so much had to be planned to accommodate him, I naturally became highly organized in other areas. Now that he has not lived at home for almost three years, I find myself more free and spontaneous, although that is a recent development. It's almost as if I had been in a locked room for so long that I didn't notice that the door had actually been unlocked for a long time. All I had to do was open it and walk through.

I can also look back with the luxury that past perspective allows and wonder why I allowed myself to be locked into certain roles for so long. Perhaps the only answer is that it was easier just to do it than to expend energy to negotiate other possibilities.

I notice my feeling of confinement returning when I have Chris home for a weekend or vacation. I enjoy being with him, and we have fun together playing games, feeding the ducks, shooting baskets, playing miniature golf, or going shopping. However, I feel again the pressure of twenty-four-hour responsibility. I can't call up a friend to go out for a movie or dinner unless I make arrangements for someone to care for Chris. I have to allow extra time to get ready for church because I have to help him dress too. I'm back into the mode of a parent who has a young child, even though I am, chronologically, past that time in my life.

My personal role shifts when Chris is at home. The other boys help when they are here, in that they also make accommodations to be with him. If we were not flexible, we would develop conflicts over Chris's visits home. If my sons viewed caregiving or meal preparation or cleaning as my domain only, I would probably come to dread Chris's visits home because I would feel as if I were being placed in that room with a locked door.

From the time you first know of your child's disability, your family must evaluate and reevaluate family roles. Try to prevent creating fixed roles, which will inhibit mental and spiritual growth in both adults and children. Be sensitive to your own needs and to the needs of the other family members. If you feel trapped, talk to your spouse and to your other children, if they are old enough to understand. Ask them to help you with tasks, or ask them to help you gain perspective. If you see someone else in your family becoming

57

trapped in a fixed role, talk to the family about it to see if you can find some alternatives. Taking the time to relieve each other's pressure will go a long way to prevent resentment and alienation. When someone has helped you carry your load, thank the person, acknowledging that you noticed what he or she did for you.

LEARN TO EXPECT THE UNEXPECTED

When we received a diagnosis for Chris, I didn't expect to become a "public" family. I never realized that I would be telling so many people about our particular situation. I knew that Chris received some stares and comments from strangers when we went out, but I wasn't aware that the curiosity would increase as he grew older. Sometimes the curiosity has a negative effect; when Chris himself notices that people are looking at him, he becomes uncomfortable and responds with a sideways look and a comment to the person, particularly if the person is a child or adolescent. However, if someone approaches us and says hello, he is gracious and responds appropriately.

Sometimes the attention is positive, although I may not realize it at the time. Someone from a church we used to attend told me that she enjoyed watching our family in church because she could see the love and caring that we had for Chris. A neighbor commented on how she loved to watch all of our boys playing baseball together on the street because she saw how Chris's brothers protected him and always included him. People are edified when they see love in action.

I'm always jolted a bit when I become aware that people are watching us. Other families have problems, such as abuse, addictions, runaways, or infidelities. But these problems are usually not visible, and our other family problems similarly remained obscured. A child with an obvious disability is immediately marked and is more likely to be scrutinized. When the disability is "hidden," as in a learning disability, the family doesn't become labeled usually until the child is in school. Unless the child has an accompanying behavioral problem, the family will not be identified in settings outside of school.

Another aspect of becoming a "public" family is the loss of some autonomy and self-sufficiency. Suddenly many people are interfering, so to speak, in your family life. In addition to receiving normal advice from friends and relatives about child rearing, you have professionals examining how you are raising and caring for your child. It can be an intimidating experience. In a sense, you become accountable to professionals for how you administer medications, schedule feeding times, do physical therapy exercises, and how you parent in general. You may begin to doubt your own capabilities in the process.

CHANGE IN PROFESSIONAL CARE

You can also expect change in your interactions with medical and human-service professionals. In the course of your child's life, you may need to interact with many different professionals: neurologists, geneticists, orthopedic surgeons, physical therapists, lab technicians, social workers, school administrators, to name only a few. You may see some of these people only occasionally for a consultation.

Although your primary-care physician may be the same person over a period of years, some of these other professionals will come and go. Positions and departments change and modify often. Each time you come for help, you need to establish a relationship with a new person. This can lead to a sense of insecurity at a time when you desperately need some sort of stability. You begin to feel as if you are walking on the deck of a pitching ship much of the time.

CHANGES IN PERCEPTION OF CHURCH

Living with a disabled child may also lead you to alter your concept of God and of church. In their book *Ministry with Families in Flux,* Olson and Leonard suggest that a change from a monarchical, totalitarian view of God to that of a loving God will benefit families of a child with disabilities. God loves us and wants us to be in communion with him, but he doesn't force us to do so.

> So we affirm that God does not send disability to test a family's faith or improve its character. Yet we also affirm that by God's grace a family's faith and character may be strengthened as they struggle to cope. God does not ordain disability in one person so that others may learn what is really important in life. Yet, through God's grace, facing the challenge of disability can redirect family priorities beyond the magic consumerism of American life. God does not permit disabilities in order to teach spiritual lessons, or expose social evils, or make a place for miracles. Yet through God's grace, spiritual truths will be learned in the presence of human vulnerability; disability advocates will arise to challenge evil; and caring medical and educational personnel will work all manner of miracles.[1]

You as a family may change your expectations of your church community. You may have been content to be only a participant in Sunday services, or perhaps you have been active in ministry. In either event, you may now be looking for more from your church pastor and congregation in emotional support, caring, understanding, or actual help with the child. If you find that these aren't available in your church, you may stop attending church or look for another.

MOURNING YOUR LOST CHILD

When a child is born, you expect to feel joy and happiness, not grief and loss. However, when your child is born with a disability or when your child is diagnosed with one, you need to grieve for the loss of the child that you had expected. In a sense, you have lost a child, even though your child is still alive. Admitting this is a difficult step.

If you don't allow yourself to grieve for the lost child, you may end up not accepting the child that *is;* you may not recognize your child's needs or accept your child's limitations.

This happened to Cliff and Mary. They couldn't face the loss of the little girl whom they had hoped for, and they denied their daughter's limitations. They went from doctor to doctor, looking for a diagnosis they could accept. They couldn't bear the term "mental retardation," so they searched for someone who would tell them she was only "learning disabled."

If your child has a disability that is diagnosed with devices such as lab reports, X rays, and CAT scans, you may find the diagnosis easier to accept. But even then, you may not deal realistically with the condition and demand more from your child than the disability allows.

Be careful not to get into a situation in which you try to fulfill your need to have as perfect a child as possible and deny the reality. If that happens, you are unconsciously meeting your own needs and ignoring your child's needs.

As I mentioned earlier, when I was pregnant with Chris, I had hopes that our two oldest children, who would be close in age, would be buddies for each other. I visualized my husband walking along the beach with a little guy on each side of him, running and playing along the water's edge. That vision died when Chris was not walking according to the expected time frame and when the developmental distance between the two brothers widened as they grew older. At the time I didn't understand that I needed to mourn that loss, the loss of the child I had dreamed about. Not until Chris was ten years old did I learn that I would have to put the "lost" Chris to rest and totally accept the Chris that I had.

I wish that I had learned that lesson earlier because it would have been easier for me to deal with his behavior problems at home. I thought that if I worked with him enough, I could make him understand how to behave. I had some idea of his limits, and I accepted the diagnosis in my head, but it took many years to travel to my heart.

INTERNAL CHANGES

My acceptance of Chris came through a time of internal crisis. Several significant events led to my crisis point. In 1976, Chris had come home from the Devereaux School after having been there for two years. Jim was deployed on a cruise, and I was caring for the four boys: ages eleven, ten, five, and two. At that time, Chris was functioning on the level of a two-and-a-half-year-old. I had no relative closer than four hundred miles and no help with the house or children. Life was very busy and hectic.

In May, another Navy wife who also had four boys joined me and our four boys for a Mother's Day picnic. We went to a park with a nice lake and paddle boats. My oldest son was off playing with her older boys, and I was having a frantic time trying to manage the three others. Chris was not being cooperative at all, and my friend told me that I looked as if I was heading for a nervous breakdown. I knew deep down that she was right.

I was, and still am, a very self-reliant person, partly as the result of my father's death when I was thirteen; as the older sister, I had moved into adulthood quickly. I needed that strength to survive as a Navy wife and to handle home and family alone. But I had come to the end of my self-reliance. I needed help.

The first answer came in the form of a friend who invited me to attend a prayer group that she and her husband were attending. She had described the group as "life giving," and if there was anything I needed at the time, it was life. I agreed to go with her sometime.

At the same time, some of the officers' wives on my husband's ship were meeting for a weekly Bible study. As a Catholic, I felt very wary of meeting with this group of non-Catholics. I also felt rather cocky about my knowledge of Scripture and didn't think that I had anything to learn. However, they were featuring weekly speakers in this group, and someone told me that the next speaker would speak about disciplining children. Since I was at the end of my rope with my own children, I thought that perhaps someone had the magic answer for me, so I attended the group, well armed with my sixteen years of formal Catholic education.

I don't remember what I heard that day about discipline, but I do remember that these women conveyed a peace and love that I wanted. As I was leaving, the hostess asked me if I had ever considered putting my hands on Chris's head and praying for him. That was such a novel idea that it was like a breakthrough. To pray for him! I had prayed, when I would think of it, for me, for strength to handle the boys while their father was away, but I never thought of praying for Chris directly.

I decided that perhaps this group was okay. Besides, they had baby-sitting, and I could get a morning off from the kids and spend the time relaxing with some nice people. I made a silent commitment to continue with this group.

Next, I decided to investigate the prayer group my friend had invited me to attend. The first night I attended, a young seminarian was speaking about Jesus as the Lord of your life. I was fascinated because I had never heard these words spoken in church. After his talk and a time of prayer in the group, I went up to him and asked him what he was talking about. I explained that I had been a church member all my life, but I hadn't heard about this before. He asked me if I had made Jesus my Lord. I had to respond that I really didn't know.

When he asked me if I would like to make that decision, I replied, "I guess so." He then asked a few members of the group to pray over me with him, and I made a verbal commitment to the Lord. I was overwhelmed with the feeling of love that these strangers conveyed to me. I wanted to know more about that kind of love and how it operated. I desired to have that kind of love in my life. That was on a Monday night.

I went back to the Tuesday-morning group with news that, to me, was still a wonder. The women smiled knowingly and were happy for me. I must have been like a child who just discovered Christmas morning, I was so enthusiastic.

I delved into the Bible, and it suddenly made sense. When I had tried in previous years to read Scripture, I hadn't understood much except the parables. Bible reading had been a chore. But now it was a delight. I learned to sit and pray and listen for the Lord speaking to me. My previous prayers had been one-way communication—me to God—and it had never occurred to me that God talked back!

I had been so independent that God had sent me *two* groups of people to help move me toward him. It felt as if God was tapping me on both shoulders and asking me if I was tired of handling this all myself. It didn't take me long to say, "I give up." Through prayer I learned that I could turn everything over to God. I could lay down my burdens, especially Chris.

God gave me a beautiful gift during those early months of my Christian experience. I had always been afraid of what would happen to Chris if I died or for some other reason couldn't take care of him. I kept visualizing a lonely, perhaps neglected, retarded adult who had no joy in his life. In one prayer time I had the sense that God was saying to me that I was not to worry about Chris anymore. He loved Chris more than I ever could, and his love was greater than my mother love. He reminded me that he had created Chris, and he assured me he would provide for him always. I was Chris's temporary caregiver here on earth, but Chris belonged to God. His love would provide more than I ever could.

The relief and joy that I felt with that revelation and promise was tremendous. I came to realize that I had to accept Chris as he was and trust in God. I began to look at Chris with new eyes. This was not a child who just "happened"; Chris's life had a purpose. It didn't matter that I didn't know the details of God's plan; but I felt assured that he had one, and we were part of it.

With this acceptance of Christ as the Lord of my life came an equally significant acceptance of Chris—just as he was. I could now put to rest the longing and desire for the "other Chris," the one who was not mentally retarded.

While I can say that I have, in essence, buried the "other Chris," life with my Chris did not become easy. Once I received the Lord's assurance of provision for Chris, daily life did not take a dramatic turn. I had to go through, and am still going through, what all parents of children with disabilities face. I have had to continue to train and teach him, to work through problems with school and community agencies. I still lack certain knowledge about his future placement. When he is home on visits, I must still choose activities carefully and adapt my normal routine.

Chris will always need someone to assist him in living and to look out for his best interests. I now can accept the role of "forever parent" without bitterness, anger, or despair. I trust in God's promise of provision, even though I don't know the details. I have an inner peace that someone else besides me is guiding Chris's life. I don't feel that I have to have total control or be the source of all knowledge and wisdom regarding him.

In my enthusiasm as a new Christian, I would pray and believe for total healing of Chris. I would try to imagine what he would look like if he was not retarded—how he would sound when we talked, how he would interact with his brothers, what he would be doing for a career. Balance came into my prayers as I matured in Christ, and I realized that I had to put the fantasy of the idealized, "normal" adult Chris to rest also. If God chose to heal Chris, it would be wonderful. But if God chose to work other ways, then I could accept that also. I learned to become thankful for small steps of progress. The people who were of such help to Chris were also sent by God, I believe, people such as inspired and dedicated teachers, caring respite-care workers, and Special Olympics coaches. Chris has touched and been touched by many lives, and that I believe is also part of God's plan.

God didn't *cause* Chris's mental retardation any more than he caused my father to die, my brother to have a serious illness, or my husband and me to divorce. But in all of those events, God is there, sending grace and constant redemption. God has created us with a range of emotions, and to say that some events don't cause sadness and grief would be to deny God's work. To feel is to be truly alive.

But God has also given us ways to work through the sadness and experience joy. As a cross-stitch picture that hangs in my office says, "The soul would have no rainbow had the eye no tear."

Jesus wept in Gethsemane and experienced a horrible death so that he would rise victoriously. We also must die to be reborn, and sometimes our dying and rising is a daily process. I don't have a complete explanation of why God designed human life in this manner. I can only observe that it is so.

Knowing this calls me to make a choice of how I will respond. My decision has been to die to my own aspirations for what I would have liked in a son called Christopher and accept the person God sent instead. I have made a commitment to "give thanks in all circumstances" rather than to despair over my situation. I can approach Chris's future with a sense of wonder and thanksgiving, knowing that provision is already there and that what God provides will be better for Chris than what I could ever devise alone.

I can rest in the assurance that one day I will meet the "other Chris"—fulfilled, whole, and complete—and we will spend eternity praising God together.

4

MANAGING LIFE

The family of a child with special needs has an enormous task—to maintain as normal a family life as possible with a family member who does not conform with expected normal family development. The family longs for balance so that it can progress, yet it always seems to be out of balance because of this child.

I'm aware of all of the important markers of my sons' lives, yet I seem to measure our family's timetable by events surrounding Chris. I can relate the dates and times of his developmental progress—walking, toilet training, learning to tie his shoes—more accurately than I can that of the other children. I know that they learned to do all of these things, but perhaps their accomplishing them was expected. With Chris, his being able to achieve was a great relief and joy—one more thing he could do.

I count the years by where Chris was in school. I didn't

realize how focused I had been on his singular achievements until I sat down to write this book. It's not that the other children didn't matter—they did, very much—but I knew that they would be able to do those things. With Chris, I was never sure, so his successes became victories.

BE PREPARED FOR CONFUSION

You will need to change your ideas of family life, bending so that you don't break. A sign on a bulletin board in our secretary's office announces, "Blessed are the flexible, for they shall not be bent out of shape." This woman has the right idea for preserving sanity.

One of the certainties in parenting a child with special needs is *you will face confusion*. You probably have no previous role models for parenting a child with special needs, unless you have seen disabilities in your childhood family.

Your feelings will be confused. You will experience love, guilt, and anger all mixed together in raising this child. You may feel trapped by total responsibility but uncertain how to progress next. You may feel frustrated at loving the child so much that it hurts yet feel defeated at the child's lack of progress.

In the wonderful movie *My Left Foot,* Christy Brown's mother says to him, "You have me heartbroken. Sometimes I think you are my heart. If I could give you my legs, I'd take yours." Many parents would willingly give anything they could to help their disabled child. Their agony is that their intense love and willingness to sacrifice can't change the child's condition.

FACING UNRESOLVED ISSUES

In addition to the confusion of not having clear guidelines for parenting the child with special needs, you will always have a degree of ambiguity. Some issues will recur in varying intensities throughout your life.

An example of this is chronic sorrow. This grieving that never ends has been identified in the studies of families of children with disabilities. I spoke earlier of mourning the child that was not and putting him or her to rest. That can be done. But chronic sorrow is for the child that exists. I can best describe it as a heaviness of heart, a sadness for the child. It may lie dormant for a while, but it resurrects at significant times. For example, a few years ago our oldest son was married. I felt intense joy as I watched two wonderful young people publicly pledge their love and commitment to each other. I felt so privileged to be a part of their lives that day. However, I also experienced sorrow as I thought of Chris.

Chris was not present at the wedding. It took place in the bride's hometown, two hundred miles from our home, and circumstances were such that we decided not to have Chris present. I had mixed feelings: I missed his presence, but I was relieved that I didn't have responsibility for him and could focus on being mother of the groom and enjoying the day.

As I watched the ceremony, I thought about how I would never be at Chris's wedding. At age twenty-five he has no idea of what a date is, although he does have female friends. He is dependent on others to provide a social structure for him.

I had the same type of feeling when Chris and I would sit in the bleachers at the ball park, summer after summer, and watch his brothers play baseball. Chris participates in Special Olympics, but it's not the same as being a part of a team and having the neighborhood people cheer you on. Again, Chris is limited to what others in his family and the community can provide for his recreation.

I suspect that the sorrow I carry is harder for me than it is for Chris. My awareness is heightened, but he lives in a different reality. He didn't know that he missed the wedding. He accepted that his role at the baseball games was of fan and spectator, and that was fun for him. My task is to keep his perspective in mind and not let my own sorrow take over.

DEALING WITH UNRESOLVED ISSUES FROM YOUR PAST

I have been discussing parents of a child with special needs in a somewhat artificial setting. The assumption is that both parents are mentally and physically healthy, functioning individuals with a happy marriage, with no other problems in life, such as finances, career, aging parents, or other children. In real life, however, these parents are like all other people, with their own set of problems and issues, only one of which is a child with special needs.

One issue that may affect your parenting of your child with special needs is unfinished business from your family of origin. You may think that once you have married and moved away from your parents, the work is done. It is more likely that you have put issues on hold, and when you face problems with your spouse and children, you may need to explore your family history.

I was discussing some school problems with parents of a child with learning disabilities. The mother said, "We are both very responsible people—we have always been that way." I suggested that they might want to explore that issue in marriage counseling; how did they both get to feel overly responsible and how was that affecting their distress over their son's problems? Their own feelings of responsibility had moved this couple into taking responsibility for their son's poor grades in school. They, in turn, were unhappy, and now the responsibility for the couple's happiness had been shifted to their son. If he would only have good grades, he could make Mom and Dad happy.

Chances are, some dysfunctional patterns in their own family of origin had precipitated overresponsibility in both of these parents. Responsibility is the balance; both irresponsibility and overresponsibility are dysfunctional manifestations that do not originate with the child with a disability but have roots in the parents' own childhood.

One of the ways to manage the confusion and frustration that arise in everyday life is to be secure in yourself and understand your own motivations. To feel that you are in control of yourself, rather than that your past is controlling you, gives you the ability to take care of your child's needs and make decisions regarding that child.

WHAT DOES IT MEAN
TO BE A PARENT NOW?

Nothing I had experienced in my life prepared me to be a parent of a child with disabilities. I had grown up with Mom and Dad setting the family rules and taking responsibility for the family. I had few encounters with "professionals" except for my family doctor, teachers, and church pastors. When Dad died, I knew that Mom had some official dealings with the Veterans Association and Social Security, but for the most part, our family was a separate entity, and the parents had the responsibility and rule.

That was the model I carried into my own mothering. I was totally unprepared for the loss of my parental autonomy when

I began dealing with outside systems regarding Chris. The number of organizations that were involved amazed me. As rounds of interviews progressed through the years, I became aware that in some respects my abilities as a parent were seemingly on trial. It was as if my fitness as a mother was being judged. I had not experienced this with my first child, and I sometimes felt resentful.

Over the years, my files about Chris have grown by inches. You probably have similar files. The reports vary, often according to the expertise of the person doing the reporting. One that I now find amusing, after recovering from the initial anger, stated that Chris was more advanced in his verbal skills than his motor skills. The reason given for this was that his mother, who is educated, places a higher priority on verbal ability and does not reward the motor accomplishments. This was an explanation for Chris' inability to ride a tricycle until he was seven years old. The absurdity in this report is that he had accomplished too much in one area, and it was my fault!

You may feel that you are often in no-win situations with professionals. Sometimes it seems that someone can always find fault with what you do. If you push for diagnosis, you are aggressive; if you sit back and watch, you are passive or negligent. When you insist that the community or school provide services, you are looked on as a pest; but when you don't band together with other parents to push for services, you are called complacent and uninterested. When you bring in charts of your observations of your child's behavior, you may be seen as thorough; but you may also be viewed as threatening or too anxious.

The perceived loss of autonomy in parenting plus the feeling that your parenting is always up for scrutiny can combine and set up several possible dynamics. One is that you feel you never win; you are always in a one-down position with professionals. Other alternatives are hostility, loss of self-esteem, resentment, and withdrawal.

It has been a struggle for me to maintain my parental autonomy throughout the years. I've had to make decisions and choices that involved taking risks in several areas. Deciding that I knew my child better than anyone else was a major choice. This is advice that I give to other parents and a maxim that I teach my students. Parents need specific help and feedback at various points, but they usually know their child best. When I deal with professionals, I approach meetings from a cooperative aspect. They are the experts in their field, I am the expert on my son, and we will work together in matching our collective wisdom to reach the best solution for whatever situation we are discussing.

I don't mean to sound arrogant when I state that I am the expert on my son. What I am implying by that statement is that the caring parent has had to work through establishing the daily routine, knows what does and doesn't work, and knows the child's likes and dislikes. That is valuable information that should be part of all considerations. The parent is the clearinghouse of years of gathered information. The parent is the guardian of the child's whole person, not just the isolated issue that may be discussed in a single meeting.

Another part of being a parent of a child with special needs is taking on roles for which you were not prepared. It came as a surprise to me that I would have to be so involved with Chris's education. This realization didn't come on me until Chris had been in public school for a few years. With the other children, I helped with their homework when needed, checked that they had everything they needed for school, and attended parent conferences as they arose. Their curriculum was set by the school, it was satisfactory, and I could be content with working as a PTA volunteer and supporting the boys' efforts.

With Chris, I had to learn how to be a parent of a child in special education. My signature said that I approved of the Individualized Education Plan. I was in the role of *advocate* for my child. I came to learn that advocacy extended beyond school; it was part of all the other services that Chris required, and it seems that it will never end.

Another change in my idea of what it meant to be a parent was that I found I couldn't parent alone. I needed other parents' help. Most parents share problems about children and ask friends' advice and support from time to time. However, the individual parent or set of parents has difficulty if he or she chooses to remain a loner. The systems that are in place for children of disabilities require a great deal of parental knowledge and initiative. You have to learn the system in order to be able to use it effectively. That requires getting to know others who can help you thread your way through what often appears to be a jungle.

The systems that serve children with disabilities often are overburdened, underfunded, and understaffed. It's somewhat paradoxical that parents, who need the services for their children, are the first ones called on to supplement and support the services. Parents who need relief and help are frequently called on to provide that relief and help. Expectations are that "interested" parents are those who pitch in and keep the systems going. I didn't mind taking my turn in Cub Scouts or baseball for my other sons. I don't mind giving my time for organizations that influence Chris's life. The difference, however, is that my participation in my other sons' activities was time-limited. With Chris, I will be expected to participate forever.

To manage this burden of participation, I've had to make

choices about what I will and will not be involved in. I've had to recognize my own time and energy limits and give myself permission to sit out occasionally without feeling guilty. Again, it's an issue of maintaining my own autonomy in as many areas as I can while staying cooperative.

You may find such a lack of services that you will have to form groups to help each other. At a parent conference a few years ago, many people from the western part of Virginia were saying that they had no access to respite services, and finding a baby-sitter for their child was impossible. Those parents may have to use their time and energy to find other parents in the same situation and work out some sort of cooperative venture. Their unique problem was that they live in a sparsely populated rural area and didn't know any other parents. This didn't mean that their situation was hopeless; if this goal was a high priority for these parents, then they would find the means to attain it. Whatever these parents chose to do—create their own group, lobby and press agencies to meet their needs, or live with the present situation and do nothing more—they remain in a situation that requires extraordinary efforts in parenting.

If you don't stop to examine what is really happening in the family, to ask some significant questions, you will drift through the days, weeks, months, and years and then find yourself surprised at your final destination, perhaps not where you had intended to go at all. You will have to decide how much you can manage to examine and change at one time, and not all areas will be universally applicable. The last thing I intend is to make you feel guilty for not being in total control of your destiny; that's impossible for anyone. But I do want to encourage you to pick and choose what you feel you can manage at the time.

You may benefit from asking yourself the following questions:

- Why am I doing the things I'm doing?
- What should I be doing instead?
- Do I have any options in my situation?
- What would I really like to be able to do?
- How can I attain what is important to me?
- What do I really not have to do?
- What would happen if I eliminated some things?
- Am I paying attention to everyone in this family (my spouse and the other children)?
- Who usually does what?
- Who else could do some of these things?
- Who would be able and willing to take on something different?
- Who outside of the family could help me with some things?
- Can I afford to pay for some outside help?
- Can I afford not to pay for some outside help?
- Whose needs aren't being met in the family?
- What steps do I have to take to meet that person's needs?
- Where are we as a family?
- Where would we like to be?
- What will it take for us to get there?

PART II

HUSBANDS, WIVES, BROTHERS, SISTERS

5

PARENTS AND SIBLINGS

I was driving home from work one day when I saw in front of me a bird walking across the road. I was going slowly, but I knew I couldn't brake safely and avoid the bird. I found myself shouting at the bird, "Don't you know you can *fly?* Why are you walking across the road?" Fortunately, the bird made it to the other side, but I was left wondering why birds choose to walk and not fly across busy roads.

Are you ever like that bird? Do you get so locked into your roles that you forget that you're also a married couple? Do you forget that you're an adult with needs of your own?

Children—especially if one of them has special needs—can easily become the central focus in your life. You lose sight of the couple relationship that needs fostering and nurturing too. When the child's special needs are intense, the likelihood of sacrificing husband-wife roles is even greater.

The actual divorce rate among families of children with

disabilities is unknown. Estimates indicate that it may be the same as in the rest of the population or it may be as much as ten times as high. In addition, no statistics give an accurate picture of divorce affecting children with disabilities; however, we do know some information about single-person households.

In 1988, 6.9 percent of all U.S. family households were headed by females with no spouse present and with their own children under age eighteen. Over 19 million persons, with an average of 3.11 persons per household, live in this situation. Males with no spouse and their own children under age eighteen represent 1.1 percent of all households. Roughly 3 million persons live in this type of household.[1]

It isn't known if more or fewer children with disabilities are in single-parent households. Using the accepted statistic for mental retardation at about 3 percent of all children, we can calculate the number of children with mental retardation in single-parent households. It would be 390,000 children with mental retardation living with single females and 60,000 with single males.

It seems paradoxical that families of children with special needs would divorce; one might think that the special needs of the child would be a unifying element for the couple remaining together. However, in a fragile marriage, the stress produced by the child's needs may be the one extra component that leads to the end of the marriage. A marriage faces so many complexities over time that it's difficult to pinpoint the exact cause of a breakup. Each family has its unique combination of circumstances that contribute to the overall atmosphere. The following list includes some of the many ingredients to consider. You will be able to add other variables that have a direct influence on your family life.

- the individuals themselves, what they bring of their past into the marriage
- the stability and strength of the individuals
- the maturity level of the individuals
- the strength of the relationship before the child was born
- the health, educational, and financial circumstances of the couple
- the number, ages, and gender of other children in the family
- the strength of the faith of the couple
- the social supports for the family
- the community services that will help care for the child

I mentioned that having a child with a disability would seem to be a reason for a couple's remaining together. In my case, that may have been the incentive that kept me in the situation for twenty-five years. When Jim and I had problems over the years, we were able to reach solutions that allowed daily life to continue as a family. It wasn't until Chris had completed public school and was in a residential situation that I discovered how empty our marriage really was. I thought that when we were freed from the twenty-four-hour care of Chris, we would have time to do things as a couple and also with the two younger boys, such as going away for weekends and longer vacations. That illusion was shattered when my husband had no interest in those things and I saw, for the first time, the empty shell of our marriage. I won't go into the details of how things came to an end, but for my own part I knew that as my focus was shifted away from Chris and more on myself and the marriage, reality hit hard. I knew that it was time to make choices and admit what I had been so successful in denying all along—mutual commitment didn't exist.

NURTURE YOUR MARRIAGE

What does it take for a couple to stay together? Many experts may word it differently, but the basic requirements are *open communication, shared decision making,* and *nurturing of fidelity, commitment, and trust.*

In many ways these components can't be separated. Open communication won't happen without love and trust. Shared decision making won't happen without mutual trust and open communication. Each element *needs* the others at the same time that it *fosters* the others. It's an ongoing process.

The New Testament makes it clear that husbands and wives are to submit to each other mutually. The ability to negotiate roles and share decision making is an example of mutual submission. With love and respect for each other, spouses will make decisions with the other's good in mind. They can then be united in their approach to deciding what is best for their children.

When a child has special needs, a family's ability to make decisions may have several constraints. Circumstances often limit what a family can do. Financial and medical constrictions are most limiting of all. Usually, however, there are some choices in the situation. I once heard it said that stress is the inability to make a decision. I also know that stress is feeling that you have no part in making a decision.

Sometimes we get so caught up in daily life that we forget that we have options. Joyce Maynard, in one of her weekly columns, commented about this topic. She said that she told her husband she was resentful of his taking off on Saturday morning bike rides with his friends while she stayed home with the children. His response to her was to ask her what she would do with a Saturday morning to herself. She was so used to her role a caregiver that she couldn't even think of a response.[2]

Couples who have foundations of trust need to nurture that trust. Trust doesn't come naturally. It's the result of thoughtful, intentional work. How can you and your spouse nurture trust?

Spouses who can't turn to each other often seek other ways to numb their pain. Often they will go outside the marriage and develop dysfunctional ways of coping. This can be another person, but it can also be other activities that are held to be legitimate in our society. Spouses may turn to excessive work or a busy schedule of church and community activities. Nothing is wrong with wanting to excel at work or volunteering in your church or community. However, when those activities are escapes from what is happening at home, they are dysfunctional. If these activities become substitutes for talking to each other about the conditions and concerns of home, if they blot out reality and give an excuse to be away physically or emotionally, then problems are brewing.

Children need parents who are secure enough in themselves to be nurturers. Parents crippled by their own distress and sadness can't nurture their children. Children with special needs require extra amounts of cherishing, support, and encouragement. The reserves needed for that extraordinary effort can come from the strength of the couple's relationship. To build that strength, the couple has to take time for each other. This sounds like an impossible task, but it isn't insurmountable. If both partners realize the importance of caring for their relationship, they will take time for each other. I have found that in my own life when I say, "I don't have time for that," what I am really saying is, "That isn't a priority for me, and I'm not going to do it." What I value, I have time to do.

Take Time for Yourself

You may think that you can't possibly find time for yourself when you have young children. Finances are often strained, and fatigue is often present. But you can treat yourselves occasionally to putting the children to bed early, ordering a pizza, and watching a video together. You might have to choose a walk in the park because the available entertainment money is paying for a baby-sitter. Spend a weekend in a local hotel if that's all the vacation you can afford. The key is that you feel that your marriage relationship is a priority and you make a commitment to pay attention to each other on a regular schedule of some sort.

Another way to develop intimacy as a couple is a cooperative spirit in childcare and home management. When each of you is willing to be an equal participant in a mutual concern, you convey a message that says, "I'm in this with you all the way." I notice fathers in church holding their young babies, and it says to me that times are changing. These fathers have their hearts invested in their wives and children because they are willing to be active participants in childcare. They don't see childcare as the woman's "job"; their love isn't confined to roles.

One of Murphy's laws is that when something has to be done, there is always something else that has to be done first. A couple shouldn't be shopping for a new car until they have both looked at their finances, needs, wants, and plans for the future and decided if a new car is the right thing to do. Parents may be arguing over which private school is best for their child without asking the question of whether or not they should be removing the child from the public school.

It's easy to become so engrossed in care and concern for your child with special needs that you forget who you are.

You talk about yourself in relation to your child. Your plans, hopes, and dreams tend to focus on what is happening with that child. Your jobs, careers, residences, and vacations are all dependent on some need of the child. You may find yourself choosing your friends on the basis of who accepts your child. You select a few certain families with whom you can enjoy social occasions. If there aren't many people who fit those categories, you can become isolated.

For example, you may not have much choice in the purchase of a family car because it may have to be a specially equipped van. Your furniture and household layout may have to be geared to the mobility of your child. Parental time off from work or vacations may be scheduled around the child's hospitalizations or surgeries. As you contend with these pressures daily, you may lose your sense of being a couple.

Handling Crises

Times of crises can pull a family together or break it apart. A couple with a strong, steady marriage has a better chance of weathering a crisis than one that doesn't. Susan Speileberg, a parent of a fifteen-year-old son who is severely mentally retarded, spoke at a Virginia conference in 1983. She commented on the stresses of the family: "I refuse to be one of those martyred parents or bleeding hearts, what I call 'do gooders,' you will have to forgive me, that sees the birth of a handicapped child as either the test of a parent's tenacity by a supreme being or a blessing bestowed by that same supreme being. No supreme being that I would want to recognize would demand the type of hell on earth that many mentally retarded children and their families live through. . . . I say retarded families because there is no family into which a mentally retarded child was born that doesn't concurrently have a mental health problem, a theological problem, a service

87

acquisition problem, and frequently an exacerbated financial problem."[3]

All parents dealing with a special-needs child experience their own degree of "hell." They also realize their own degree of hope and heaven, and sometimes all can occur on the same day! The incredible stress produced by the child's needs creates demands on a couple that exceed the normal by several degrees. Given these circumstances, it would seem that the couple must work on developing their relationship to be a bonded, strong pair and thus be able to withstand the strains that now exist and are yet to come. Neglecting that precious relationship may lead to disaster.

This book can't possibly discuss all the aspects of marital strength and happiness, but I would like to highlight some potential problems that arise in dealing with the child with special needs. If you can spot a problem area early, you may be able to commit yourself to working the issue through so that it doesn't become the straw that breaks the back of your marriage.

Blaming for the cause of the child's disability. One spouse may blame the other as the reason for the child's problem. If either used drugs or alcohol prior to or, for the mother, during the pregnancy, blame may be attributed. If there is a genetic disorder, one spouse may also try to identify the other's genes as being at fault. The father may lay blame on the mother for improper diet or too much exercise or working too late up until the time of delivery. Without talking through the matter and attempting to reach some understanding together about the cause of the child's disability (if a cause can be found), blaming will drive a wedge through the relationship.

Blaming for the child's misbehavior. One spouse may not approve of the other spouse's style of discipline and will hold that spouse responsible for the child's behavioral difficulties. "She's too easy" or "He's too tough" may be common complaints. Lack of consistency, unwillingness to enforce discipline, or harsh discipline may also be issues that create blaming. If this is a problem area for you, try to sit down together and work things through to present a united front to the child. Not only will the child have a better opportunity to improve behavior when both of you clearly state how you both expect the same behavior and both enforce rules consistently, but the child will no longer be able to play one off of the other, as children have a great ability to do.

Taking on guilt. Parents have a marvelous facility for taking on the total responsibility for their child's problems, even when it is illogical to do so. When a parent acts out of guilt, everything that is done with and for the child is colored by the guilt. The other spouse can become secondary in the quest to meet all the special needs of the child.

Financial stress. Parents may find themselves bearing a tremendous financial burden for health care. All of the available insurance money may by used up by the child's medical needs. One parent may have to quit work to care for the child, and the other may have to take on a second job. I think that financial realities can be one of the greatest tests of a couple's commitment to one another. It's much easier to carry on life when you have sufficient resources; when trying to keep food on the table becomes difficult, a couple is sorely tested. I don't mean to sound simplistic, but perhaps this is one area where a couple may find it easier to call on their faith to rise above the circumstances and keep them hopeful. I don't have a sound knowledge base for that statement, but I do know that I hear our university students testify how time and time again God provides finances just when they need it. I've seen God's financial provision in my own life, and I've seen it in our church's. Money doesn't seem to be much of a problem for God. (But then, what is big for God?) Perhaps the issue is that some things are too big for our own ability to believe.

Responsibility for daily life. The responsibility issue really has three parts: taking it on, delegating it, and abandoning it. Who does what and when is part of the whole decision-making process that has to occur in the family. Often the balance of responsibility is unequally divided around the care of the child with special needs. That lack of balance, paradoxically, may be what is keeping the false balance in the family. When one person, usually the mother, attempts to delegate caretaking responsibilities, the balance may be so upset that chaos may result. Here again, sitting down to talk together about the best approach to handling the long list of responsibilities may prevent a disaster in the future.

Relating to in-laws. Everyone is aware of the gamut of problems a couple encounters with in-laws. Some couples lack a united stance toward their own parents. When a couple has a child with a special need, they may face potential divisive problems with the child's grandparents. For many, the grandparents may be a source of both emotional and practical support. However, if they are non-supportive and interfere, blame, deny, and project feelings, the couple may face a dilemma. Spouses may feel a divided loyalty—between their own parents and their spouse. They may want to help their own parents with grieving and pain over the disability of their grandchild, but in doing so they may be asked to align with the grandparents in blaming or finding fault with their spouse because that will meet the grandparents' needs for absolution of blame. The issues become compounded. The couple must stand together so that they are not divided.

You face a lifetime of ongoing changes with your child. What won't change, however, unless you actively choose to do so, is the fact that you are married to one another, and together you are responsible for your child. If you wish to remain a couple and have a fulfilling marriage, you must work at open communication, shared decision making, and nurturing of fidelity, commitment, and trust so that you can deal with the many aspects of life with your child.

THE FAMILY AS A SYSTEM

When discussing a child with a disability, we must discuss the entire family as a system. Each family member is affected in some way by the disabled child, and the child is affected by each family member. In past years, research was conducted only on mothers of children with disabilities. Recently, fathers, grandparents, and siblings are being included in research, although we still don't have extensive research on grandparents and siblings.

We also must keep in mind that each family is different, and the effect of the child with a disability on the family members varies by several factors:

- composition of the family itself;
- age, gender, and birth order of each child;
- economic and social position of the parents;
- educational level of the parents;
- support networks in place for the family; and
- philosophical/religious beliefs of the family.

Also, the high rate of divorce causes another focus, not only of the single-parent family but of the effect of stepparents, stepsiblings, and possible half-siblings. When there is a divorce, the mother is most often granted custody of the child with the disability. Future research, perhaps, will pay attention to the interaction of mothers and children and noncustodial fathers.

If families are aware of some research findings, they can be aware of what is happening in their own families and use that information to enhance their own family life. Research has shown that having a child with a disability can be a positive or a negative influence on the family, and often there are elements of both. The family, particularly the parents, can choose courses of action that can emphasize the positive while accepting the seemingly negative.

I often think of concentration-camp prisoner Victor Frankl, who while he was literally stripped of all clothing and possessions yet was able to state that he could never be stripped of the way he would choose to react to such circumstances. We need to be aware that we *can choose how to react* in our situations. This enables us to deal with some tough situations and yet recognize the needs of all of the children in a family, not just the one with overwhelming needs. The following story is an example of dealing with one such situation.

It was a pleasant summer afternoon and Bill and Carol Jefferson and their three children (ages ten, twelve, and thirteen) were on a family outing to a large theme park. This was a special trip because the park was a two-hour drive from their new home, and it was their first visit. Also, the youngest child was finally tall enough to ride the adult rides, and it would be the first time the family had been able to enjoy the rides together. Admission was fairly expensive, so the family would be able to go only once that season. The family planned carefully for this trip, packing a lunch to save money and discussing "strategy" so that they would ride the more popular rides early in the day to avoid long lines.

The family plans went awry, however, as they were boarding the first ride, the small roller coaster. Twelve-year-old Patricia, who had an unspecified developmental disability, suddenly began protesting aloud that she didn't want to ride and stiffened her body so that she couldn't be helped into the car of the roller coaster. Carol led her back through the line to a nearby bench while Bill and the two boys went on the ride. Patricia didn't want to ride many rides that day. The only thing that interested her was the train, the merry-go-round, and the rides for younger children.

Carol spent the day taking Patricia on the rides she preferred. She had to convince operators of the kiddie rides to allow Patricia to ride, even though she was larger than the other children. Bill took the boys on all of the rides they chose, and the family met together to share the picnic lunch. Even though the boys enjoyed the rides and the day, the activity wasn't a family event. Carol and Patricia were separated from the others, and Carol didn't get to enjoy any of the rides.

The next year the family planned a similar outing. However, they used a respite-care provider for Patricia, and Bill and Carol enjoyed the day together with their sons. Patricia participated in other activities that summer through a therapeutic recreation program, including horseback riding and an overnight camp-out.

Parents of a child with special needs are always working a balancing act to provide for the needs of all of the children. Often difficult decisions must be made, and it's hard to know the right thing to do. The Jefferson family thought that

Patricia would enjoy the outing at the park. She had seen it advertised on television, and the family had been talking about it for weeks before. Patricia had been on some rides at county fairs and enjoyed them. Bill and Carol had no idea that Patricia would balk at the roller coaster. They had to decide whether to try it again the next year and hope that Patricia would feel more comfortable or not to include her so that they and the boys would enjoy the day. They made their decision and felt comfortable with it.

They also might have considered other options. One would have been to include Patricia, let her ride the rides she felt comfortable with, and have Bill, Carol, and the boys take turns being with her. Another would be to have a companion or respite worker come along and take Patricia on the rides she wanted, with all of them meeting from time to time. Or Bill could take their sons to the theme park alone and Carol would stay home with Patricia.

What is important is how the family arrived at the decision. Allow all family members to be involved in the discussion, and find the solution that meets the most needs.

CHARACTERISTICS OF SIBLINGS

Research studies give us some valuable insights into the siblings of children with disabilities.

- Older siblings adjust better than younger children do to having a brother or sister with disabilities, with the exception of the eldest daughter, who doesn't adjust as well.
- Eldest daughters often are given the task of caring for the child with special needs, much more often than do any other children in the family.

94

- Children are more affected by having a sibling with a disability if that sibling is of the same gender.
- If there are only two children in the family and if the non-disabled sibling is a girl, she suffers more adverse effects.
- If there are only two children in the family and one has a disability, the other is more pressured to fulfill the parents' hopes and dreams for success in their children. If the non-disabled child is a girl, she is also assigned more caregiving responsibility.
- Siblings of children with disabilities tend to show positive qualities of being well-adjusted, mature beyond their years, tolerant of differences in people, helpful toward people, and aware of social needs.
- Siblings can be excellent teachers of their brothers and sisters with disabilities because they are in a different position in the family.
- Siblings may judge the worth of their friends by the friends' reactions to their brother or sister with the disability.
- Siblings may experience guilt as they surpass a disabled younger brother or sister in skills and abilities.
- The siblings may feel pressure to overachieve.
- Siblings may overidentify with a mildly disabled brother or sister or may, as they reach teen years, not consider a severely disabled sibling a person.
- Siblings may feel that requests by parents for help with the brother or sister with a disability to be either an intrusion on their time, or they may view it as a privilege to cooperate with the parents.[4]

ROLES OF SIBLINGS

At the 1990 national conference of the American Association on Mental Retardation, not one seminar in the five-day conference dealt specifically with siblings. This is an interesting phenomenon because the role of siblings in the life of a person with disabilities is increasing. Because of advanced technology in neonatal nurseries, many more disabled children now survive birth and come home to live with brothers and sisters. Children with impairments that would have been cause for institutionalization in the past are now cared for in their homes, where siblings are a very real part of their lives, and vice versa.

Also, more adults with disabilities are living in the community. Many are remaining in their parents' homes, and others are living in some type of group home in the community. If these disabled adults live normal life spans, they will outlive their parents, which may mean a sibling will need to act as the case manager for the adult with disabilities.

The possible long-term involvement of siblings with a disabled child is only one issue of many that are important to consider. The siblings aren't just the "other children." All the members of the family are part of the family system, and we can't talk about one child without talking about everyone in the family. Twenty years ago, I was advised to put my son into an institution and concentrate on my other child. No one even thought of what might happen to my other child, who, if he had never met his brother, might have faced a difficult situation later on. For example, Charles's parents institutionalized his brother, James, when James was an infant. Charles only recently found out about James's existence. Charles is faced with a set of difficult decisions: Do I now enter into James's life? What good would it do? I'm too far away to even visit. Would James understand or would I be a stranger? Would James be upset to find out about me and not be able to come to live with me?

We have to consider our families as systems and remember that what happens to one of us happens, in some way, to all of us. When we think in those terms, it not only affects our decision making but also our communication with the other children about what is happening. Considering the family as a system may lead us to include the other children as part of the decision-making process when appropriate.

CHRONIC SORROW IN SIBLINGS

I spoke earlier about the aspect of chronic sorrow in the parents and of their mourning the loss of the child they had hoped for. We also must consider the siblings' losses as well. Elizabeth Wein wrote the following eight years after her brother, Jared, then age eleven, was severely brain-damaged in an auto accident:

Neither I nor Jared has yet learned to accept the way he is. If anything, the acceptance gets harder as we grow older. He is nineteen now. His former friends—none of whom have stayed in touch with him—all graduated from high school last year. As children we were very close, and since Jared's accident we have been drifting further and further apart. I grow older, Jared stays the same. I can't properly "mourn" him because he isn't dead; but the healthy, active, intellectual boy who was my brother before 1978 is dead. If I could accept the youth who is handicapped, who occupies so much of my life as a different person, it would be easier for me. I can do neither of these things. Jared as a child and Jared now may be different, but he is still a single person.[5]

97

Not only did my dream of my sons being buddies for each other die, but Jimmy, our oldest son, recently mentioned to me that he missed having Chris as that buddy. He told me that he used to think of how neat it would be to have a brother in the same school, close in age, to do things with, and to look out for him. Jimmy felt the same loss I felt, only in a different manner.

SEVERITY OF THE DISABILITY
AND ITS EFFECTS

Another area that is yet to be explored is how the severity of the disability affects siblings. At first we may think that the more severe the disability, the more severe the effect. However, that isn't always true. A child with a visible, severe disability, such as JeanAnne, who has cerebral palsy and is in a wheelchair, is clearly seen as having an impairment. When her sisters are out in public with her and she expresses herself in a loud, garbled word, people may look toward her wheelchair and be understanding. However, when Bruce, who has no readily apparent sign of disability, is out with his family and makes the same sound to express himself because he is nonverbal, people look at him and aren't as understanding. Bruce's brother and sister may feel far more embarrassment in public situations than do JeanAnne's sisters.

Also, because Bruce, although nonverbal, has no physical disabilities, his parents expect him to participate with his brother and sisters in some recreation and play activities. His brother and sister may be resentful at having to include him. They also feel more frustrated because Bruce isn't able to keep up with them, even though he appears to be physically able to. They expect him to have the self-control appropriate for his chronological age, even though they know that he has a developmental delay and is in special classes. Bruce's siblings may experience guilt for feeling embarrassed or being ashamed of his behavior when they are out with him.

How parents respond to their child with a disability communicates to their other children what having this child means to the family. If the family centers on the child, the other children may conclude that they aren't valued. If a balance is reached, where everyone's needs are considered, then the message is that each person is important to the family. In that context, granting some concessions to accommodate the child with the special needs also can give a signal to the other children that they, too, will always be accepted as part of the family, just for themselves, and not for their accomplishments. When Bill and Carol Jefferson arranged for a respite-care worker to be with Patricia while they took their sons to the amusement park, they were telling their children that each individual in the family was important, and that they, as parents, wanted each to have fun.

PARENTING STYLES

Parenting styles can be examined from two aspects—how the parents deal with the child with a disability and then how the parents deal with the other children in the family. Generally, but not always, parents will be consistent with their parenting styles and beliefs about children. What may differ is the matter of degree. Of course, it's always possible that a parent will be very paternalistic about the child with the disability and then cavalier about the other children, almost to the point of ignoring them. Any combination is possible with human beings. However, for the most part, we parent with one basic style and add on some features from others.

The Getaway

The "getaway" parent removes himself or herself either physically or mentally from the situation. While we all need to get away at times, this parent consistently abdicates responsibility for acting in the situation. Problems with children are viewed as unsolvable, and the parent chooses to escape. This parent may read, work, watch television, or just be absent from the house, especially in times of crisis. The getaway parent delays discussing issues because of the belief that someone else should be filling the vacuum that pulling away creates. This parent probably doesn't have a close relationship with the child.

Children with this type of parent aren't taught how to communicate and share feelings because this parent doesn't want to hear anything. To hear it means that it has to be dealt with, and this parent will escape to avoid dealing with real issues.

The Commander

The "commander" parent views the child as helpless, one who must be directed and ruled. This parent uses power to make children conform to established standards, which are usually set by the parents. This parent doesn't view the child as having any rights. The child is told, "You're not doing it right" or "Why are you so stupid?" The name of the game here is win-lose, with the parent always winning and the child always losing. This parent identifies with the child closely, seeing the child as an extension of himself or herself, and therefore as one to be molded in the parental image. The main disciplinary tool of this parent is punishment. Communication with this parent is likely to be one-way: the parent tells the child what to do. The only communication from the child to the parent is when the child says what the parent wants to hear.

The Victim

The "victim" parent takes on the role of a suffering martyr to the family. The child is viewed as a burden to be endured. This parent overworks, rarely asks for or accepts help, but doesn't fail to alert everyone as to how overburdened he or she is. In fact, no one can suffer as well or as much as this person. This parent has a number of physical ailments, either real or imagined, and generates pity by telling everyone all of his or her problems. The victim parent uses guilt, which often works, but can backfire. The guilt can cause others to fight back and build defenses.

The victim parent doesn't recognize his or her own needs, putting everyone else's needs first. The result is resentment toward people who don't reciprocate. Children in this situation feel guilty. They are deprived of the opportunity to do things for themselves. Communication with this parent often consists in being told what will happen and what has been provided without any input being asked of the child. The child has no chance to participate in decision making because everything has already been taken care of, for the child's own good, the victim parent would say.

The Entertainer

The "entertainer" parent views the child as unhappy and sees himself or herself as a playmate. The parent wants the child to like him or her and avoids unpleasant problems. This parent is nonjudgmental and allows the child complete freedom; in addition, this parent wouldn't expect the child to work through any unpleasant circumstances for the child's own good, such as painful physical therapy. The cavalier style of this parent would smooth over any bad feelings by providing an escape mechanism for the child, such as an entertaining experience. Communication with this parent is likely to be limited to pleasurable topics only; "Don't feel that way" or "Forget about it and keep on going" are phrases that this parent will use when the child brings up what are considered unpleasant topics, such as anger and fear.

The Dynamic Parent

The "dynamic" parent is committed to the growth, independence, and long-range development of the child. The child is viewed as a person with potential, a person who is in the process of training and progressing toward adulthood. The parent realizes that children have civil rights and views the child as having participatory rights in the working of the family. The dynamic parent encourages children's input where appropriate for the level of the child's ability. This parent builds the child's skills and the child's self-esteem. Communication in this family is open. No subjects are taboo, and everyone's voice is heard and considered. Decisions are made after listening to everyone's opinion. Parents hold the responsibility for making the decision, but they consider the welfare of the whole family. In this atmosphere, children learn to grow and expand their abilities and horizons. Calculated risk taking is allowed, which means that parents look at all options and then decide if it is safe for the child to proceed.

Communication skills are central to family interaction. The dynamic parenting style allows open, two-way communication that focuses on the relationship of parent and child. Dynamic parents foster acceptance and inclusion of the child with sharing of information, ideas, feelings, and knowledge. When these parents correct, they focus on behavior, not the person.

The other parenting styles tend to breed closed communication, which is destructive and blocks growth. Children are judged, excluded, and may feel unloved or rejected. When getaways, commanders, victims, and entertainers correct their children, the focus is on the child not the behavior, which keeps children immature and prevents them from taking on appropriate responsibility.

PARENTAL SKILLS FOR NURTURING

Parents can use some specific skills to help all of the children in a family where a child has a disability. They can use *empathy* by asking themselves, "How would I feel if I were this child's age?" It's so easy to forget what it was like to be a child. Not only that, but today's children grow up in a world very different from the world their parents had to face. Not only are family structures much different, but society has changed very much in attitudes, morals, values, and economic expectations.

The next skill helpful for parents is *involvement*. All children should be included in family discussions. They should know the nature of the brother or sister's disability, the prognosis, and the plans for the future. Information given to the children should be appropriate to their age and understanding. A younger child won't understand medical terminology but can be taught the name of the disorder; the full meaning of a disorder can then be explained later as the child is able to absorb and understand. The same concept applies to discussing the future of the child with the disability. When the children are young, it's enough for them to know that you have made provisions for all of them through a will and through choosing guardians. Later, as they are older, specifics can be discussed, such as where will the brother or sister work or live, who will manage details, and the exact nature of the finances, for all of the children.

Parents can also *share* their feelings, knowledge, and ideas. By sharing, parents communicate to children that they are human and give the children permission to be human also. They don't have to maintain a façade of always being right, in control, and perfect. They can share that they also feel worries and fears as well as joy. Sharing is a valuable component in faith, which is caught, not taught, to a large degree. We can tell children to believe in God, but it's our faith in action that they observe and learn. Admitting human emotions allows God to be God and allows parents to convey a realistic impression of what faith is all about.

Parents who *send clear messages* to their children are doing them a great favor. Their words and actions are always congruent. (Saying "I love you" with a frown is an example of a muddied message.) Parents also need to be simple and direct with younger children. When we give children messages, we should always ask for some kind of feedback. When I phone someone and a child takes the message, I always ask the child to repeat the message to me so that I can be certain it has been written down correctly (if at all). Feedback confirms that the child has received the message that was sent.

Parents also need to *listen* to their children in an active manner. They can give their children verbal rewards; they look and sound interested. They use long pauses, nods of the head, and "uh-hums" to acknowledge that what the child says is important. A child who is listened to feels valued in the family.

When parents use these communication skills, they present the notion that they are maintaining a balance in the family, that everyone is equally important. The parents are fostering teamwork, cooperation, creativity, flexibility, and joint problem solving and planning. Parents who operate in this manner have made a decision not to allow a disability to control the family. Other children aren't ignored, and the needs of the child with a disability aren't put above the needs of everyone else by one or both parents. Others aren't expected to sacrifice themselves for the sake of the child with special needs.

THE BALANCED FAMILY

When parents work at keeping the family in balance, they promote optimism and harmony as opposed to pessimism, tension, and conflict. The husband and wife are in balance; the parents and children are in balance; and the family itself is in balance with others.

The following suggestions may help families improve family relationships, increase the self-esteem of all children in the family, and provide additional learning opportunities for the child with special needs.

- Don't compare your children to each other.
- Be consistent in your expectations of behavior for all the children. For example, don't accept behavior like temper tantrums from the child with special needs if you don't allow it in the other children.
- Encourage each child to develop an identity, strengthen abilities, and pursue individual interests.
- Role play situations with the siblings so that they can practice responses to others' comments and questions about the child with the disability.
- Make an effort to have siblings' friends in the home to interact in limited situations with the child with special needs. Summer was a good time for our family to do this because the children could all swim and shoot basketball together—two of Chris's strengths.

- "Catch" your children in positive interactions with their brother or sister with special needs and praise them for it. Let them know that you observe and appreciate what they do.
- Recognize when you are sliding into an unproductive parenting style, such as commanding. Pay attention to your own emotions and talk through what happened with your spouse or a friend. If you can look at your own behavior objectively, you've made the first step toward change.
- Don't always wait until your children have a problem to find out how they are feeling about something. Use story time or play time, particularly with younger children, to role play. You might also read specific stories and ask the children what they would do in the situation or act out situations with puppets or dolls.
- Be real with your children. Allow them to see you laugh and cry or be grumpy or joyous. Let them know why you are feeling as you do.
- Allow your children to express negative feelings about their sibling with special needs. It's okay for them to feel impatient, discouraged, or frustrated occasionally. Let them know that you understand and that they need not feel guilty or ashamed for having these feelings.

6

THE SINGLE PARENT

When I decided to include a chapter about parents who were single, I had no idea that I would be sailing in such uncharted waters. It isn't unusual to be a single parent of a child with special needs. However, little has been written about the topic. I researched two data bases that include a variety of professional journals and conference presentations and found virtually no information about the topic.

As I began to explore the subject mentally, I reflected that the word "single" could apply to a wide array of situations. It can apply to someone who has never been married or to someone who has lost a spouse because of death, legal separation, or divorce. The single parent who has gone through a separation or divorce may be a custodial, non-custodial, or joint-custodial parent, and even these situations would vary if one of the partners had remarried. A parent may be "situationally single," with a spouse gone for long periods of time for business, military duty, illness, or incarceration.

Because one chapter can't begin to address all of these dimensions of life as a single parent with a disabled child, I have chosen to deal with the issue of the single custodial parent, when the separation is due to death or divorce. As I was preparing to write this chapter, I began thinking about my own experience as a single parent, as a divorced parent, with legal custody of my son who has a disability. However, I realized that my experience with single parents reached into my childhood; my father died when I was thirteen, making me a child of a single parent. When I was married and my husband was in the military, we were separated one-third of our married life. The separations varied from a few days to ten months at a time. While I had financial support of a husband, in the day-to-day responsibilities, I was indeed a single parent.

Some of the most difficult times as a single parent were medical emergencies, handling discipline, and the general chaos of living as the only adult in a household of children. My standard joke was that sometimes the day's "score" was Lions, 4—Christian, 0 (the children being the lions and I the Christian). Even though I was married, Jim was often thousands of miles away, sometimes in the middle of the ocean and not accessible.

DEATH AND DIVORCE

The single custodial parent has unique needs. The end of the marriage, whether through death or divorce, brings a time of mourning. This process can include shock, denial, and anger.

Divorce and death both involve losses, but the situations differ in several significant aspects. In death, there is public announcement and people come together for some sort of ceremony. Friends, relatives, neighbors, and co-workers come to pay their respects. People often bring meals to the family, make donations to a memorial fund or send flowers, and write notes of condolence. Death is a natural process that happens to everyone, and society accepts the emotions of the grieving widow or widower.

In divorce, the only announcements are the ones the separating spouses choose to make or the ones other people make without the control of the separating spouses. There is no gathering-type ceremony, only legal procedures. Friends and family not comfortable with the divorce may align with one person or sometimes desert both altogether. Formal mechanisms, like a memorial fund, are not available to help people show support during a divorce, although I have seen some greeting cards that address the topic. There is also no corpse to bury, and besides grieving over the loss of the marriage, the former spouses have to find new ways to relate to each other if they both intend to be active in their children's lives. Divorce doesn't carry with it the sense of finality and closure that death brings, and except in rare cases, divorce is an adversarial process, leaving a parent involved in settling financial and custodial matters over a long period of time. All of this leads to a sense of abandonment.

When a person becomes single through either death or divorce, changes occur in more than just the marital status. The change ripples through every layer of life. But through it all, the children continue to grow and have needs. The parent is adjusting to change on two levels—being a single adult again and being a single parent.

LIFE CHANGES AND ADJUSTMENTS

Change is a threat to the child with special needs, who thrives on routine, stability, and consistency. The parent is immediately faced with a dilemma and a challenge: how to meet new circumstances while keeping the environment of the child as steady as possible. For a father or mother who had an established career, death or divorce might bring fewer changes, unless that parent's working was dependent on the other for childcare. If childcare is well established and financial arrangements are secure, then the parent may have an easier time in maintaining stability.

However, if the family was dependent on two incomes and there was a death with inadequate financial provision, the surviving spouse might have to move or make some other arrangements to get by, such as renting out a part of the house. In cases of divorce, statistically, the woman's standard of living usually decreases substantially, while the man's increases. Current laws that require equitable distribution of assets and enforcement of support payments are working to eliminate this problem.

TAKE CARE OF YOURSELF

We parents of children with special needs often forget how to take care of ourselves. We may be able to get along fine until some major stress or crisis develops. If we continue to ignore our own needs, we will suffer the consequences, mentally or physically or both. We are so used to giving priority to the needs of our children, especially our child with a disability, that we don't know where to begin to care for ourselves. When our usual support systems are gone, we may react by increasing the focus on our children, which only puts greater stress on ourselves. It's a natural reaction to want to compensate for the loss in our children's lives, whether that loss is by death or divorce. In working so hard to maintain stability for our children, we forget to keep ourselves in balance.

When Maria's husband, Bill, died after a long bout with cancer, Maria was left to care for their three young children, one of whom had some neurological problems. In an effort to deal with her grief, Maria plunged into volunteer work in her church, including developing the Sunday school program for children with special needs. She soon found herself working forty hours a week as a volunteer. She also gained weight, had episodes of high blood pressure, and was getting migraine-like headaches more frequently. With church work and caring for her children and a large house, she was tired a lot of the time. Meals were eaten at whatever fast-food restaurant was handy on the way to soccer games or dance lessons for the children. Maria's only recreation was an occasional movie and meal out with friends.

This continued for two years. One evening, Maria attended a grief support group. Maria eventually realized that her frantic activity was both a way of dealing with her grief and her attempt to keep her children busy and involved so that they didn't have to talk about their grief. Her Sunday school efforts were really a way of making sure that her church provided Bible education that she felt her son couldn't get in regular classes because of his learning problems.

Maria discovered she needed to step back and take a look at her life. If she was to be an effective mother, she needed good nutrition, exercise, and proper rest. In addition, she needed to think about her future—she couldn't be a church volunteer forever. She began exploring possibilities for a career and decided to begin by taking a few courses in women's studies to learn more about herself before deciding what to pursue. She also learned how to manage her time to allow her to achieve her goals. Fortunately, Maria had a house and insurance money that allowed her the luxury of time to find solutions.

For parents already working outside the home at the time of marital change, the temptation might be to become a workaholic and focus on the part of the self that is tied to the job. They may take on extra work and long hours to deal with the grief. They can neglect self-care and choose to focus only on work and the children, with unfavorable results. At some point, we all have to find places of balance—physically, mentally, intellectually, and spiritually.

LEARN TO RELY ON GOD

I would be the last person to say that I have the answers to life as a single custodial parent. However, through experience, I've found something that keeps me anchored and helps me deal with situations. That something has been a total trust and reliance on God. It sounds so simple, but I found that as I give over total control to God, things work out. I've had to make a commitment to daily prayer and time with God, not by the clock, but by the leading of the Holy Spirit. That *commitment* is the key to learning trust. It's as if that time is my well, from which I can draw strength.

It doesn't mean that I don't have to make decisions. I haven't stopped gathering information, weighing alternatives, and taking responsibility for my actions and decisions. Occasionally I still feel hassled or experience stress. But as life unfolds, events seem to fall into place in a way that I couldn't have ordained myself. I also have a peace about decisions that I make.

In some ways, God's provision is unexplainable in words. One has to experience it to know what it is about. I haven't been transformed into a perfect person, and my life isn't always wonderful. But trusting in God has given me a strength that I don't have on my own and the peace that truly passes all understanding.

THE SINGLE-AGAIN PARENT

The "single-again" parent has a number of tasks to perform regarding the child with special needs.

- Not only must you deal with your own emotions about the event, but you must answer your child's questions and deal with his or her emotions. Children aren't very good at articulating how they feel, but they do act out their feelings. Since you, the custodial parent, are the closest available person, you may be the target of the child's sadness, anger, rage, or confusion. If the child has a disability that impedes understanding, the process is a more difficult one. Depending on the child's level of understanding, he or she may never fully grasp the reality of the situation. Perhaps the most the child will comprehend is that "Mom and Dad now have two houses, and you can visit Dad in his house as often as you like."
- Learning to be a single-again parent involves a shift in understanding who you are. It can be a tremendous opportunity for personal growth. One shift you may find yourself making is in your model of parenting. You may have to change from being an adult in charge to forming a team with all the children. It isn't fair to force the children into adult roles, but you can reach a harmony in which everyone shares in roles and functions, especially in the care of the child with special needs. You have to

keep the ultimate responsibility for household affairs, but you can delegate tasks and encourage cooperation.

- You may need to call on extended family members or close friends to share some childcare activities. You may find it difficult to ask for help and even more difficult to entrust your child to others who may use childcare methods different from yours. However, increased adult support may give you a needed lift.
- You may wonder if anyone of the opposite gender will ever be interested in becoming involved with a person who is the parent of a child with special needs. Facing the reality of limited possibilities in a future partner because of your child may be difficult. If you do begin to date, it may be difficult to find baby-sitting or respite care, so you might have to contact other parents and trade off hours of care.
- In response to being single again, you may become too protective, indulgent, or controlling of the child with special needs. You need to plan for your own free time, to interact with other single parents, to be realistic about expectations you have about your child, to be practical, flexible, and persistent.
- You must allow yourself the luxury to make mistakes. When you do make a mistake, and you will, it's important to count your losses, assess your gains, and move on. Remaining stuck at the place where you beat yourself over the head for being imperfect is counterproductive for both you and your child.
- Be sensitive to the child who has lost a same-sex role model. Organizations such as Big Brothers or Big Sisters may be of value to provide that role model. One summer I hired a friend's teenage son to be a companion to my little boys, to give them some recreational time with an

older male while their dad was on cruise for several months.

- Be especially sensitive to the stresses that build up inside you; if your coping mechanisms fail, you could become physically abusive to the child. If you find yourself hitting your children or getting out of control when you spank them, get help immediately. Call a private therapist or local mental-health service. Groups such as Parents Anonymous can help you with your stress and help you develop other means of discipline.

- Avoid responding to loneliness—either your own or your child's—by sharing a bed with a child. Allowing a small child to snuggle with you occasionally may be suitable, but establishing a practice of sleeping together may be stepping into dangerous territory.

- You may find that your grief, loss, and anger affects your interactions with others. When you are in disagreement with professionals about your child, you may not feel emotionally strong enough to state your position and discuss the situation to resolution. You may withdraw and allow the situation to continue, or you may overreact with inappropriate emotional force and make demands. If you feel unable to deal with the circumstance in a manner that will be beneficial to your child, ask for help. Seek out an advocate from a disability-related group or a local human-services agency. State offices have disability advocates who can give advice. You might ask another parent to help you sort through a situation or even attend a meeting with professionals. Be direct with professionals about your own situation. It isn't a weakness to admit that you aren't at your best; it takes courage to ask another person for understanding and help.

- Your child needs *both* parents to remain involved in his or her life. This may be difficult for you if the situation between you and your former spouse is tense. One suggestion I found helpful was to approach a former spouse in a somewhat professional way. View your interactions about the child as you would any other conference. Call to set up an appointment, bring a written list of what is to be discussed, and jot down what is decided. Keep the situation businesslike and focused on the child's welfare. Remember that you don't have to respond to all statements or questions at the time of the conference. You can ask for time to gather more information and promise to get back to your former spouse with a reply within a reasonable time. In the meantime, you can check out a matter with your lawyer if you are unsure. Former spouses need to refrain from pushing each other's "battle buttons"—those topics that bring emotional responses and resurrect old fights. It's crucial to keep out of the former spouse's arguments, to deflect and ignore inflammatory statements. Be aware of your own reactions to what formerly might have been a topic of contention, and control your own response if that subject is raised. If your disabled child is young, you may not have as many matters of discussion unless there are medical problems. But as the child grows, you will need to discuss many issues: vocational plans, residential plans after school is over, and financial planning for the child. You will have to find acceptable ways to remain connected, for the sake of the child.

CUSTODY OF THE CHILD

An issue for divorced parents is custody. The history of custody is that from medieval England through colonial

America, the husband owned the farm, house, and children, with no consideration for the fitness of the father, reasons for the divorce, or suitability of the situation for the children. Eventually, this was recognized as being harsh, and a practice of awarding mothers custody of children of "Tender Years" evolved and was expanded in the late 1880s to the model of seeing the mother as the caretaker and the father as breadwinner. During the Industrial Revolution, fathers worked long hours away from home, and mothers generally stayed home, although many women and children worked in mills and factories. In a divorce, the father left, and the mother kept home and children.

For a long time this automatic custody to the mother was the practice, but new models are evolving. More courts are recognizing joint custody and liberal visitation rights.

A custody decision for a child with special needs may be very involved. The child may require a level of care that one parent alone can't give, especially if that parent is employed outside the home. In Virginia, the child-support formula is based on income and number of children. A parent who is desiring custody will have to alert his or her lawyer to the circumstances and calculate what will be needed for respite care or perhaps a care attendant. Medical coverage for the child and arrangements for the future should also be written into the divorce agreement.

When choosing a lawyer, find a person who will be knowledgeable about children with specials needs and applicable laws, such as Social Security laws. Don't be afraid to ask local organizations for referrals and to then call lawyers and ask for a fifteen-minute interview so that you can make an informed decision. Choosing a lawyer in a divorce case should be done with almost the same degree of consideration that you would use in choosing another spouse; you must be compatible and have each other's trust. Divorce settlements affect you for the rest of your life, and you must be thorough. If your lawyer isn't familiar with the needs of children with special needs, you may not feel confident that your best interests are being served.

BUILDING YOUR NETWORKS

Being single again means that you will be making decisions by yourself, not only for you but also for your children. Even if you were the person who made most of the decisions about your child's education or medical treatment when you were married, chances are you still discussed them with your spouse and felt that you at least had another adult who shared responsibility. Now you may find that a good deal of the decisions are yours alone. This is certainly true if a spouse has died; it may or may not be true if there is a divorce. The feeling of total responsibility can be overwhelming. Just as you can call on others for physical care of your child, you can develop some trusted friendships with people who understand your child's situation and consult with them. Those friends may be other parents, your child's teachers, or just friends from other areas of your life. What is crucial is that you don't try to bear burdens alone. If taking charge seems like too much on a given day or if you're not sure how to handle a situation, ask for help. There is, indeed, wisdom in a multitude of counselors.

In inviting others to become part of your life regarding your child with a disability, you are also opening yourself to new forms of relationships. If your former spouse was your only confidante, you may discover many people who are now available to you and who are willing to share your life. This may come as a revelation if you were used to keeping family business strictly in the family and not telling others about your life. I'm not advocating that you should tell everyone all of your private business. What I'm saying is that you can take some risks with people with whom you feel comfortable and who share some of your concerns about your child. I'm always surprised that when sharing about Chris with a relative stranger, often that person will tell me about a relative or close friend who has a disability. I receive understanding, compassion, and sometimes some helpful advice.

EFFECTIVE PROBLEM SOLVING

As a single-again parent, you may find that you are experiencing some blocks in solving problems as a result of the death or divorce. Sometimes you are unaware of the reasons behind the inability to be effective in a given situation. Often you think you have resolved issues, only to become stuck, without knowing why. You know that you need to take action, yet you find you keep procrastinating.

Tom knew he had to see his lawyer and revise his will after he was divorced. He was aware that his children should be named as beneficiaries of his estate and that he had to insure their future. However, he kept making and cancelling appointments with his lawyer. Seeing his indecision, Tom's sister, Joanne, remarked, "This wouldn't have anything to do with who will be named guardian of the children, will it?" When Tom and his former wife had made a will, they had had a quarrel over who would be the children's guardians. His wife insisted on her parents being named because they were well off financially and lived a very stable lifestyle. Tom felt that his wife's parents doted on their son but weren't as interested in his daughter, who required special education and would need some guidance all of her life. Tom had wanted

Joanne to be named guardian; she was a teacher, and although she wasn't married, she would have been able to provide what both children needed. Tom didn't want to resurrect the battle again, because he and his former wife had joint custody, and he knew he would have to discuss this with her.

Once Tom identified the problem, he was able to discuss it with his lawyer, who then suggested a meeting with Tom, his former wife, and her lawyer. The four of them worked out a solution that gave Joanne custody if both Tom and his former wife were to die, and his former wife's parents would have liberal visitation privileges, including having the children for summer vacations. This arrangement gave Tom a sense of peace, knowing that the children would be provided for while they were young. He and his former wife agreed to review the stipulations of the will in five years.

While I was writing a chapter for another book, I became frozen and couldn't make progress. Rather than fight the keyboard and face another unproductive day, I decided to investigate the holdup. By taking some time to sort through things in some quiet, prayerful moments, I discovered that the topic of the chapter was connected to a very painful time in my life. I still had some residual anger and hurts that I first had to express and then put to rest. Once the process was complete, I could move on and write.

ANGER AND FORGIVENESS

Recognizing what is obstructing your progress or preventing you from effective action is the first step toward solving the problem. You may find some unresolved matters from your previous marriage affect how you parent your child with special needs. You may not have agreed with how your former spouse handled things, or you may have felt angry because you were deserted to handle things alone. You may be resentful toward your former spouse's indifferent attitude, or you may resent your former spouse's involvement.

Holding on to anger is unproductive. You need to forgive your spouse, but premature forgiveness only delays dealing with your problems. The following steps may help you work through a block in your life.

- First identify, clarify, and understand the anger or other emotion that is blocking your growth.
- Ask the Lord for help to see the situation with supernatural eyes, entrusting the matter to Providence.
- Accept whatever part you may have had (such as not taking a firm stand or being passive) even if you weren't the "wrongdoer." Ask for the Lord's guidance to help you put it all aside.
- Ask for understanding of how not to carry this any further into your life, to consider it finished and buried.
- Seek guidance on how to relate in new ways to your former spouse, to stay out of old emotional entanglements, and work for the good of the child.
- Bring the issue of forgiving your former spouse to the Lord, asking for the right circumstances and time frame.

Working through unresolved problems can free you to be a more effective parent, to make the decisions that you will have to face for your child, and to have peace in your own life.[1]

PART III

FROM INFANCY TO ADULTHOOD

7

PARENTING INFANTS AND TODDLERS

I was incredibly unprepared for the phenomenon of being a first-time parent. I had taken courses in child development for an elementary-education degree. I had done some baby-sitting and had helped with my younger brother, but nothing prepared me for what it *felt* like to be a new mother. The changes in my body before and after the birth and the requirements of caring for an infant were all new and unexpected.

PARENTING AN INFANT WITH A DISABILITY

I often wondered what it would have been like had Chris been my first child. I can't imagine having to deal with a baby with extraordinary needs as well as my own newness at parenting. On all levels—physical, emotional, spiritual—I believe I would have reacted very differently from how I reacted to Chris as a second child. Many parents do have to cope with their first child having a disability, and they have my respect.

Fathers also traverse a path of emotional change. Husbands are concerned for their wives' health and well-being at the time of delivery and afterward. Consider, then, what the father feels as he discovers their infant has special needs, that things will not be what they had expected them to be: "This child will require so much. Will we be able to provide what she needs? Can we afford the medical care? How much time will my wife have to spend in caring for this child? Will we ever have time for ourselves as a couple again?"

Both of you as parents are further propelled into a world for which you are unprepared, a world in which your child becomes a "case," in which you and your child are now "clients" or "patients." You may encounter strange language—technical and medical terms or professional jargon—which you will learn to decipher and eventually speak fluidly yourselves. You may find yourself dealing with many more people than the normal obstetrician and pediatrician. You and your child may now require a team comprised of specialists in many fields.

New Roles in Parenting

You may find that the circumstance of becoming parents of an infant with special needs has thrust you into a role that you never could have imagined. You may have to make weighty decisions in the first weeks and months, such as authorizing surgery for your infant. You may be expected to educate yourselves quickly on your child's disability. One father was handed brochures on Down Syndrome when his son was born and asked to read them and share them with his wife. He saw pictures of children who to him appeared to be deformed, and he threw the pamphlets away without reading them. It was more than he could cope with at the time, and he felt that he didn't want to upset his wife.

You may also need to play a role as team leader or case manager for your child. You may be astonished to learn that the people involved with your child don't necessarily talk to each other or see all of your child's records. You may need to take on an administrative role, as I discussed in chapter 2, keeping records and coordinating efforts and services to some degree.

Even thinking about doing all of this is overwhelming. Fortunately, you don't have to take on everything all at once. You grow into the roles gradually, executing tasks as they come into your awareness. Sometimes I think over the past and say, "If only I had . . ." But that's not very productive thinking. I didn't do all of the things that I recommend in this book. Some I did very well, and some I didn't do at all. Yes, it might have been better had I been more efficient or better educated about programs, policies, or services. I might have made different choices if I had been more aware.

But I did the best I was able to do at the time. And that's all I should expect from myself. It isn't helpful to berate myself for what I did or didn't do. I learn from my mistakes, and they help me devise more effective strategies for the future. I offer these musings to be encouraging. In some ways, parents feel totally responsible for whatever happens to their children with special needs. You need to keep a balance. As the Serenity Prayer of Alcoholics Anonymous reminds, you need to accept what can't be changed, have courage to change the things you can, and gain wisdom to know the difference.

When you believe that you can make changes or that help is needed, you must keep in mind that you aren't the only one responsible for providing what your child needs. An example of this is a couple who believed their child would benefit from a therapy called "patterning," where teams of people come into the home several times a day and physically move the child's body, particularly arms and legs, in certain proscribed ways in an attempt to train the child's brain to learn these movements so the child becomes mobile. This was a seven-day-a-week program, and many volunteers were needed. The announcement of the need was placed in several church bulletins on an ongoing basis, and a corps of volunteers emerged to do the patterning with this child. The parents didn't have to enlist people. They could allow their broad church community to help them.

It may feel like an invasion of privacy to have strangers involved with your family, but it may be a risk you'll have to take to help your child. Very few people need as extensive a network as is required for patterning, but when you have an infant with special needs, you may want some other forms of assistance. If you are spending a lot of time at the hospital, you may need help with routine matters, such as taking care of your mail, newspapers, yard work. If you belong to a church, you can ask for specific help, which makes it easier for your church family to be supportive. If your child needs medical treatment in another city, either immediately or later on, others' help will allow you to concentrate on your child's immediate needs.

A Long-Range Perspective

It's important to keep in mind that news of your child's disorder or developmental delay doesn't necessarily mean he or she will *never* do certain things. Of course, I'm looking at my own situation with the luxury of a backward perspective. For example, Chris didn't walk until he was almost two years old. At the time, I was looking at his delay from the viewpoint of a mother with a two-year-old, and I was very concerned that he wasn't walking. Now I can say that in his life as it is now, it really didn't matter whether he learned to walk at age two, three, four, or ten. The fact is, he walked, and when I watch him do the fifty-yard dash in Special Olympics, the date of his first steps loses real significance. It was only a number that indicated there was a delay, and not much more.

I have to admit, however, that in some areas, for some children, there are *nevers*. Chris probably will never get a driver's license, but so what? He can use taxis and buses. That's how I contend with the nevers. Once I've mourned and grieved and put away whatever the never is, I can then say, "so what?" Some things may just not matter. Another way I keep in touch with sanity is to say, "One hundred years from now, who will care?"

Unique Needs of Babies with Special Needs

In most areas, trust your instincts and common sense in dealing with your child's needs. For example, if your baby has a visual impairment, sew little jingle bells into the cuffs of the child's socks to encourage the baby to find his or her feet. Talk to your baby while you care for him or her; this not only facilitates language development but also lets your baby know where you are physically positioned.[1]

Babies with special needs may not be adept at communicating with you. They may not have strong cries or a well-defined variety of cries that inform you what is wrong. Babies with disabilities may be either unresponsive to their environment or overstimulated by it, exhibiting undifferentiated fussiness, crying at everything, requiring you to expend much time and patience in learning to respond to your baby.

Parenting any child is like walking on a balance beam

between two chasms—overprotection and independence. Achieving a balance with a baby who has special needs is a particularly difficult task. You probably will struggle with wanting to provide for your baby's needs but without spoiling the baby. You want your baby to feel loved, but you don't want that love to smother.

Sensitive Babies

If your baby doesn't conform to the advice found in baby books, don't be discouraged. Marilyn Segal offers help in her book *In Time and with Love,* in which she discusses several types of babies.[2] Your baby may be irritable, hard to soothe, and resistant to cuddling. You may feel your baby is rejecting you.

Some babies are hypersensitive. They are easily aroused and seem to be hyper alert. Their nervous systems are easily overloaded. If your baby is hypersensitive, you will need to control your baby's environment strictly. A room that floods with sunlight for a few hours a day may be too much for your baby to handle. Or your baby may react strongly to a bright light that is turned on when you come into the room. Keep the amount of light in the room steady by keeping a night light on at all times, and use a dimmer switch for an overhead light or lamp to increase light gradually when you come into the baby's room.

Your baby may be sensitive to noise. If so, keep the phone's bell on a low level and try to tone down the doorbell so that the baby won't be startled. You may need to consider installing acoustical tile in the ceiling and having carpeting and draperies in the house to absorb noise. Talk to your baby in a soft voice that you can increase, allowing the baby to adjust gradually to a normal speaking range.

Your baby may also be sensitive to texture. Segal suggests

keeping the same texture of blankets and sheets for the baby's crib, for example, always using all-cotton fabric. Wash new baby clothes before putting them on your baby, not only to soften them but also to remove any processing chemicals. She also recommends wearing soft clothes when you are going to be cuddling and feeding your baby.

Segal also suggests that the baby should be introduced to new experiences gradually and slowly. For example, submerging a baby in a tub bath isn't the first step, but the last. Allow the baby to get used to the depth of water by inches each day, until the feeling of water is no longer a threat.

Chris was sensitive to changes. When he was a baby, he would enjoy being pushed in his stroller. However, if I was out shopping, he enjoyed it only when we walked along the sidewalk. When I would turn to enter a store, he would cry and would continue crying until I left the store and we were again back on course. It was embarrassing to me because all eyes would lock on this screaming child. However, it saved me a great deal of money—I shopped quickly, for necessities only. He also would cry if we stopped at red lights when we were out driving in the car.

Signs of stress in your baby may not always be evident. Marilyn Segal advises parents to look for these signs of stress: a change in expression, a tightening of the lips, a curling of the toes, a slight change in skin color, hiccupping, spitting up, and bowel movements that are outside of the normal routine.[3]

Delays in Development

One of the joys of parenting is seeing the baby's "firsts," those developmental markers that tell you your baby is progressing normally. Keep in mind that "normal" encompasses a fairly wide range. If a child doesn't walk on a certain date, it doesn't necessarily spell disaster. However, if your child has passed beyond a normal time for accomplishing these tasks, you may need to consider the possibility of developmental delays. The following chart is a brief indicator of what children may be expected to accomplish at certain times.[4] All figures are given in months.

DEVELOPMENTAL STAGES

Smiling ½–3	Standing 8–16
Rolling over 2–10	Walking 8–18
Sitting alone 5–9	Talking (words) 6–14
Crawling 6–11	Talking (sentences) 14–32
Creeping 7–13	

Infant-Stimulation Programs

A delay in only one area may not be a cause for concern. However, delays in more than one area are reason to inform your pediatrician. If you feel that your observations are ignored, find another doctor who will listen to you. If your baby has developmental delays, then it is of utmost importance to enroll the baby in an infant program that will provide necessary intervention. If your doctor does not suggest or know about such a program, call your local city agency that administers services for those with developmental disabilities. If you are in a remote area or very small town, call a national information agency. The old "stitch in time saves nine" principle applies in infant-stimulation programs. Studies have shown that babies in these programs make gains that they wouldn't have, had they not been in the program. Another benefit of the program is that you are connected with other parents and learn that you aren't alone. One reason that babies in infant-stimulation programs do so well may be that you receive the confidence to continue the program activities when you are home with your baby. In seeing program workers interact with your child, you indirectly receive training that you can continue at home. Emotionally, you may feel supported and understand that investing time in the baby now may reap tremendous dividends later.

Playing with Your Baby

Interacting with your baby at home may take the form of structured and prescribed activities from an infant-stimulation program, or it may mean just taking time to play with the baby. With babies, play can always involve learning. Exercises given by a physical therapist or speech therapist can be worked in as play. Sometimes parents may feel that therapists may be demanding too much. It is okay to take a day off from physical therapy if you need to. The consistent pattern of exercise pays off in the long run, and a day off now and then may be healthier all around than going through your baby's exercises when you are feeling stressed.

Stay Encouraged

Be careful not to become obsessed by measuring your baby's progress as an indication of the value of the exercises. When you have a special-needs baby, you learn to rejoice in small amounts of progress. It's not the quantity of progress that's important but that your baby continually moves forward.

Faith enters here, because it's so easy to become discouraged. I learned that any measurement of Chris's gains would come in months, and in some cases, years. Sometimes it was only in looking back a few years that I could realize that we had come a significant distance forward. I've always had to remind myself that although I gave birth to Chris, he really belongs to God, and I'm a caregiver for a relatively brief span of time. I have to keep an eternal perspective—the ultimate in long-range planning—toward a time when we will be together always and when he will no longer have a disability. My frame of mind in those times isn't denial; I'm not avoiding the problem. Thinking this way sees me through the problems.

PARENTING A TODDLER WITH A DISABILITY

For most children, the toddler stage occurs between ages eighteen months to three years. However, for children with special needs it is more complex to define the toddler stage. To toddle means to "walk with short tottering steps in the manner of a young child," and totter implies instability and wobbling.[5]

Some children with special needs may never reach the point of walking at all, but yet they will attain toddler stage in age. On the other hand, a child may walk much later than the usual beginning of toddler age. I always associated the beginning of the toddler stage for Chris when he was twenty-two months old, because that's when he first began to walk alone. However, I have a more difficult time determining when toddler age ended for him. I think of it as around five, because that's when he achieved success in toilet training. Each parent will have a unique definition of what toddler age means for the child.

I don't have a lot of clear memories of the toddler years—I think because I was so busy and had toddlers for so long. The memories I do have are more like the thirty-second bytes on the evening news—short vignettes of events that travel through my mind. I can't recall many very happy times when Chris was in the toddler-preschool years. Not only were they busy for me physically, but I think that they were difficult for Chris. He had to make several moves of cities and residences, get used to being in programs and meeting many new people, and cope with trying to make sense of his world with limited means to do so. I think that both of us must have been unhappy for those years.

Communication with Your Toddler

One of my frustrations was an inability to communicate with Chris as I could the other children. There was much he did not understand, and if he did comprehend, he couldn't let me know that he did. Impaired or limited communication is shared universally, I believe, by parents of children with developmental disabilities, unless the child's special need involves only a physical disability that doesn't include speech and language.

Just as you had to become skillful in "reading" the cries of your baby with special needs, you also have to work hard to interpret your toddler's communication. In all children, receptive language develops before expressive language, that is, the child is able to understand what we say before he or she is able to communicate to us in similar language. In children with developmental delays, the gap between expressive and receptive language will be larger than it is in most children.

That factor compounds the problem of communicating with the child, for it's difficult to know that your child understands you when he or she can't communicate back to you. We sometimes ask children to repeat a message to us, to make sure that they understand. When the child can't do this, we have to look for other clues.

In our family, we have learned that Chris will usually say yes to the last item if we offer him two or more choices, so we now ask each question involving choice twice. "Do you want

135

chocolate or vanilla?" and "Do you want vanilla or choco-late?" When we get a consistent response, then we know what he really wants. For some unknown reason, Chris has always confused the words "off" and "on," "love" and "hate," "like" and "don't like." This mixing occurred early and has been consistent throughout his life. Because we know about it, we are alert to question him to make certain of his meaning when he uses these words.

In her book *Handicapped Infants and Children,* Carol Tingey-Michaelis discusses how to deal with children who don't understand the meaning of words.[6] She gives details of how to teach meaning to children. For example, to teach the word *ball,* a parent would present a ball to a child, roll the ball to the child, and say the word *ball* several times throughout the process. Parents should smile and say "thank you" and other verbal praises at each step.

Teaching language will require time and considerable patience. Instructing and guiding children with special needs throughout the years requires consistency, stamina, and faith that what you are doing in such seemingly small steps will, in the long run, contribute to the child's growth.

Teaching Behavior

When you help children develop language, it's easier to teach them acceptable behavior. You may become tired of being "teacher." You may have tried some things that didn't work, and you have become discouraged. Be careful not to have unrealistic expectations of yourself. You're not a behav-ior-modification or disciplinary expert.

There are no perfect parents. There are no perfect pro-grams, either. Admitting those two facts allows you to try strategies, and if they don't work with your child, then discard them. Ask other parents what works for them. Look at a number of sources, such as books, special-education teachers, and other parents, and pick and choose what seems best for you and your child.

As you try to teach your special-needs toddler behavior, keep these guidelines in mind.

- Be consistent in your discipline, and remember to praise and affirm your toddler's acceptable behavior.
- Inform the adults in the child's life about what words are understood for certain actions. For example, when Chris was young, he had no comprehension of what it meant to say, "We'll go to the beach in three days" because he didn't understand what a "day" was. However, if I said to him, "We are going to the beach in three sleeps," he knew what that meant: He would go to bed three times at night, and then we would go to the beach. We passed this information on to the rest of the family and everyone knew to talk to Chris in terms of "sleeps."
- When you give your child a request, allow sufficient time for the words to sink in. It may take your child time to process the information and act on it. If the child doesn't comply, you might want to rephrase the request. Perhaps the child doesn't want to drink the juice because he wants milk, and so you have to check out why the child isn't carrying out your request to drink juice.
- When a child doesn't comply with your request, be careful not to label the child as rebellious. Look beyond the noncompliance to other possible reasons why the child isn't behaving the way you have requested. A child who has learning disabilities or attention-deficit disorder may not be rebellious at all; he or she may not understand the request.
- Don't yield to relatives' pressure to spank your child because they think all your child needs is the "rod of

correction." Let relatives know your household rules and how you prefer to discipline your child, and then stay with your convictions.

Everyday Concerns

The toddler years may be an extension of babyhood in that parents are still working with children on tasks that are usually accomplished by age two or three: using the toilet, eating and dressing independently. Toilet training is probably the most difficult of these tasks, as it involves a sophisticated process of learning to identify signals from the body and then making a proper response. Control of the muscles required for toilet training comes late in the sequence of development. In addition, some children may have problems that hinder the process. If you are having concerns, discuss them with your pediatrician to make sure that your child has no physical problems that would hinder his or her use of the toilet. Then work patiently and consistently with your child, gaining help from books and from other parents whose children may have had similar problems.

A toddler can't continue to nurse from breast or bottle only, as requirements for nourishment change. Some children may resist foods because they don't like the texture. A recent issue of *Exceptional Parent* devoted a page to feeding suggestions. A teacher wrote about crumbling graham crackers in applesauce to get a child used to the feel of solid foods and then progressing to finger foods. Also, parents told of stroking the cheek and jaw of the child firmly with the hand and with material of different textures, such as velvet and terry cloth. They also found it helpful to rub the gums of the child with a clean, damp washcloth to stimulate the feel of texture. A hopeful note was in a letter from a parent of a twenty-one-year-old son with Down Syndrome who, although he had feeding problems when young, now comes into the kitchen and "inhales" everything in sight.[7]

Dressing is probably less of a problem now for children than it was when my children were young. Velcro has to be one of the greatest inventions for children with special needs. Velcro closings on sneakers and clothing are a major plus; they are available in stores to replace buttons and snaps if the clothing does not come with it. Also many clothes for children are now designed along the lines of sweatsuits so that even older children can be dressed comfortably and easily. Grandparents and others who buy clothing for your child may need to be alerted to looking for clothes that are easy to put on and take off.

New Symptoms, New Diagnosis

The toddler years may be a time when you are searching for a diagnosis or looking to refine and get more information about one you already have. Your child may need to have further testing, which means you and your child will be interacting with more professionals. It may also be a time when you see some vague symptoms that you are at a loss to categorize; some of these symptoms may signal a learning disability or attention-deficit disorder. However, the diagnosis of these disorders is not usually made until the child is in school and the learning deficits become apparent. For these children, the toddler years can be difficult. They may have difficulty in private preschools. If they are identified as developmentally delayed, they can attend a public-school preschool program and intervention can begin, especially in behavior, speech, and language. Children in these preschool programs are not classified in special-education categories until the age that they would usually enter school for first grade. (Special-education preschool is discussed in the next chapter.)

Parental Roles

As we discussed in earlier chapters, couples periodically need to reevaluate who does what. The toddler stage is a necessary time to examine parental roles. If the mother is particularly stressed out during these years, her husband needs to become involved in new ways. If couples take time to examine what is happening to them as their child has increasing needs and if they are aware of how they might easily slip into set roles that are a barrier to keeping them connected as a couple, then they have taken the first step to enhance their relationship. As they reconnect as a couple, their interactions with their child will improve also.

The toddler years bring complexity to the family's life. The child with special needs is requiring more services, and the family has to increase its ability to adapt to changes and to be flexible. Life contains many trade-offs. Setting priorities for the family recognizes this fact. When I decided to attend graduate school, I had to set my priorities as family and studies; everything else had to go so that I could achieve my goal. If a family recognizes that time invested in interventions with the toddler is important enough to give up something else, then they are more likely to be motivated to participate in programs that will benefit the child.

This perspective also prevents parents from locking into fixed roles. If helping the child is one of the family goals, then it's not the responsibility of mother only.

Respite Care

Your toddler may need special care if you are to be able to spend any time away from home, whether that be for an afternoon, an overnight trip, or a weekend. It's important that you trust the person caring for your child.

Respite care provides people qualified to deal with children with special needs. And because respite care is usually subsidized, you can give your child expert care at a reasonable cost.

You may be reluctant to entrust care of your child with special needs to a non-family member. Respite workers have special training, including first-aid and CPR certification. If you are doubtful about using respite care, think about the following advantages, built on the word RESPITE:

Relaxation . . .   gives families peace of mind, helps them relax, and renews their humor and energy.

Enjoyment . . .   allows families to enjoy favorite pastimes and pursue new activities.

Stability . . .   improves the family's ability to cope with daily responsibilities and maintain stability during crisis.

Preservation . . .   helps preserve the family unit and lessens the pressures that might lead to institutionalization, divorce, neglect and child abuse.

Involvement . . .   allows families to become involved in community activities and to feel less isolated.

Time off . . .   allows families to take that needed vacation, spend time together and time alone.

Enrichment . . .   makes it possible for family members to establish individual identities and enrich their own growth and development.[8]

Respite programs vary from after-school centers to summer programs to in-home care. Some charge fees and some do not. The number of hours a family may have subsidized respite care each month may vary by locality. Virginia Beach has a Rotary Respite Residence where children (infants through adults) may stay overnight or up to three weeks. The Virginia Beach Rotary gave seed money to begin this program, which is administered through the Community Services Board. The program itself was developed with the help of a parent-advisory group. One of the members of that advisory group was Sheridan Cline, who uses the residence for her three-year-old son, Kevin. In a newspaper interview, Sheridan said, "If not for respite and some of the other support services available, personally I'd lose my mind."[9]

If you are concerned that a respite worker would not know how to care for your child exactly as you do, you may want to do what Laura's mother did. With assistance from a professional, the mother created Laura's Care Book. Laura was two-and-a-half at the time and had severe respiratory problems, a rare genetic disorder, and hydrocephalus. Laura's mother took appropriate pictures of Laura in several activities, such as eating and bathing, and then wrote a one-page, step-by-step description of each activity—the procedure, the supplies the caregiver would need, where those supplies are kept, and what Laura's responses might be. Laura's mother put all of this information into a three-ring binder with separate headings. The book is accessible when Laura is being cared for in her own home and can also travel with her when needed. The book can be revised easily as Laura grows and her needs change.[10]

Church Nurseries

The church nursery presents another opportunity to interact with caregivers about your child's needs. Before you use the nursery, one parent might volunteer for a Sunday so that you could get an idea of what the situation is like. It may be that the nursery is not appropriate for your child, or it may be perfectly fine, and then you can be reassured. You should meet with the nursery worker ahead of time and introduce your child, perhaps leaving your child for only a brief time at first. It would be helpful to have a Care Book or any special requirements written on a card in the child's diaper/bottle bag, so that if there were questions, a caregiver could have ready instructions.

If the nursery is not suitable for your child, meet with your pastor (with the child) and tell of your needs. The pastor may know of someone who could help or may support you in beginning a special-needs nursery or in training current nursery volunteers to work with children with special needs.

When our church couldn't meet my needs for nursery care, I hired a sitter on Sunday mornings for about two years. This not only allowed me to attend church without worrying about Chris but also provided care for Chris's younger brother, who was too young to benefit from church yet. This might also be an occasion for parents to use respite care, so that they can remain involved in their church.

Finding Appropriate Preschool Programs

You want your toddler with special needs to have a suitable preschool program. If your child has been in an infant-stimulation program, then there will probably be a natural flow into a preschool situation. If your child is recently diagnosed, then you may be searching for a program.

Many types of preschool programs exist across the country. Some are within the public schools, with children attending daily. Some are administered by community programs, and children may attend daily or a few days a week. In community

143

programs, staff may be all professional or a combination of professional and volunteer. A program may have a home-visitation element, and some programs will have a wide range of services available to the family.

In selecting a preschool program for your child with special needs, consider these standards:

Qualified staff. The people in the program are crucial to the child's growth and development. Not only must staff persons have necessary education and certification that demonstrate the knowledge to carry out the program requirements, but they also must be caregivers who communicate understanding and love to the children. They should be ready to answer all of your questions adequately.

Physical facilities. The physical environment should meet fire and safety regulations. It should also be clean, of adequate space, inviting, and have a sufficient number of toys and necessary equipment for children.

Welcoming atmosphere. The staff should consider parents as partners in the child's education. You as well as your child should feel welcomed and invited. You should be introduced to all of the staff members, whether paid or volunteer. The schedule, details of transportation, what your child will need (diapers, change of clothing, juice cup, etc.), and the best means to communicate with the staff (at home or at the program, times to call) should be provided.

Goal setting. The staff should set clear goals and methods of assessment for your child, and you should have input into the goal setting. You should know how often your child's progress will be reviewed and be a participant in that review.

Parent interaction. The preschool should provide some means for parents to get to know each other and to meet periodically. Parent education, and ideally, parent counseling, should be a part of the program. (Most preschool programs do not include parent counseling, but it is as crucial now as in the newborn years, because of the increasing gaps in development of the child and same-age children who are progressing normally.[11])

The Family as Client

In some programs, the family is identified as the client. Does that mean you're an abnormal family? No. It represents a forward step, that of realizing that your child doesn't exist in isolation from you and your other children and that everyone in the family is affected by the child with special needs. When the family is considered as the client, the program looks at the whole picture of your family. For example, let's say that a certain preschool program is recommended for your child, but you can't consider it because you have only one car and the program doesn't provide bus service. A family approach would mean that either a case manager or program director would help you examine alternatives to secure transportation because a family goal is to have the child in preschool.

Some programs offer home-based interventions. Combined with a family-as-client approach, the clinician can help determine what you need to help your child succeed. I wish that I had had the benefit of this approach when Chris was young. A psychologist visited my house to help begin a behavioral training program for Chris, to keep him from hitting his younger brother and taking toys away. Because the focus was on the behavioral method, the other needs of the family were not investigated. I was instructed to count the number of times Chris took a toy away from his brother daily (using a golf counter) and then begin leaving Chris alone with the baby for short periods of time, gradually increasing that time.

The program failed. I couldn't feel comfortable leaving Chris alone with the baby for any time periods, and no alternatives were offered. As I look back, what I probably really needed was a mother's helper for a few hours a day, to allow me to spend some time alone with Chris, without the baby around, and also to give some help with the household chores so that I could interact with the two children together more often to teach Chris sharing behaviors.

Home-based programs can be beneficial when you are motivated and the program fits the needs of both you and your child. An advantage in a home-based program is that you can control the timing, location, and agenda. Be sure to stay open to the clinicians and other help that is offered.

IS IT WORTH IT?

It may be during your child's toddler stage that you realize the permanency of your child's condition, whether it be a learning disability or a rare genetic disorder with mental and physical impairment. You may have to count progress in your child in very small steps—even, perhaps, as just having a "normal" day without any negative incidents. You may even feel as if you are not seeing progress but taking some backward steps. As a parent who has been through the cycle of those periods several times, I encourage you that in the long run things do have a way of working out. I don't mean to sound trite, as if everything turns out happily in the end, but my perspective when Chris was three is very different now, over twenty years later. Each stage in the child's life is an important one for growth, and each stage provides an opportunity to learn of God's mercy, blessing, and provision.

Parents Are People Too

You may be a parent of a toddler, but you do not want to be a "toddling" parent—tottering in your own life. Keeping in balance physically, emotionally, and spiritually is probably one of the best preventive measures you can take to help your child through these years. Pay attention to your child's needs and provide the best that you can in the situation, but you also need to take care of yourself. Stay attuned to what God has for you at this time, taking comfort in the Word and resting on God's promises. My mother sent me a card that said, "Worrying is like a rocking chair—a lot of activity that gets you nowhere." Jesus told us, "Who of you by worrying can add a single hour to his life?" (Matt. 6:27). Sometimes you may forget that you are to enjoy your children. You think in terms of the child's special needs and forget that he or she is a child. Give yourself permission to take some "days off," to think of yourself as just a parent, your child as just a child, and enjoy the moments.

At a recent workshop I received a handout titled, "Parents' Bill of Rights," which was excerpted from *Survival Guide for People Who Have Handicaps* by Sol Gordon. The purpose of the Bill of Rights was to remind parents that they can enjoy life as just plain people; they don't always have to operate as a parent of a child with special needs. In essence, it gives parents permission to be themselves.

I have paraphrased a few of those "freedoms" for you.

- Be free to recognize that you are doing the best that you can.
- Be free to enjoy life "intensely" even though you have a child with special needs.

- Be free to allow yourself to feel angry without feeling guilty.
- Be free to enjoy being alone sometimes.
- Be free not to divulge all the details of your life and problems with your child to everyone. Sometimes just say that everything is "fine."
- Be free to be honest with your child, praising when appropriate, and letting the child know when the behavior is not pleasing.
- Be free to have your own hobbies and interests and to give time to issues and causes regarding disabilities as you choose.
- Be free to spend some extra money on yourself occasionally and to take time with your spouse for dates and vacations.

At the bottom of the handout was printed a warning, reminding parents that if they don't enjoy these freedoms, they're in trouble. Being a "martyred" parent means that you will seldom be appreciated by anyone, least of all your own child!

Acting like a martyr is a temptation for the Christian parent. We want to follow Christ's example and be selfless. We take to heart words such as, "If anyone would come after me, he must deny himself and take up his cross daily and follow me. For whoever wants to save his life will lose it, but whoever loses his life for me will save it" (Luke 9:23–24). Parents may misunderstand these verses. Christ is speaking in much broader terms than being the parent of a child with special needs. The cross is not the child. The cross represents the total giving up of ourselves to Christ in all aspects of our life. We are to give up anger, bitterness, and hatred. We must surrender our selfishness and ambition to God's will. The cross we carry is our own sin nature that keeps us from

148

cooperating with the fullness of Christ's mercy, love, and peace.

We are not called to give up what God has for us and sacrifice it for our child's needs. We have a high calling as parents of a child with a disability, to nurture, encourage, and strengthen that child. We are the ones who will give the child tools for living. We will, after all, probably be present for only a part of the child's life. Our call is not of martyr but of enabler. Taking up our cross involves allowing God to guide us and empower us for the task and putting aside our own desire to live our lives through this child or to make the child dependent on us. We may feel that it's natural to make the child the focus of our lives, to sublimate ourselves and serve the child. It's by God's grace that we can perform the more difficult task—that of helping the child reach his or her optimal potential, which is harder work. Losing our life for Christ means that we do what Christ wants, not what we want.

A POTPOURRI OF THOUGHTS

I offer you here a number of thoughts, ideas, and practical hints for coping with your baby or toddler with special needs.

- When a baby with special needs is born, you face many dilemmas. One area that may be particularly confusing is in dealing with remarks that other people make. Part of the confusion is that you may not know what you need and want from others at this time. You want people to rejoice with you over this new life. You want some acknowledgment of the disability, but you don't want pity. You may feel ambiguous in your own feelings and responses yet expect others to say the right things. It's important to keep in mind that people are generally well

149

intended but yet can appear thoughtless or may hurt your feelings. If you can take the first step and let people know how you as parents feel about this new baby and the special needs, you may put them at ease. You can also let them know that their support and encouragement, especially their prayers, are important to you. There are always those few people who will be insensitive because they are too wrapped up in their own hurts, and the best you can do is forgive them and pray for them.

- Allow yourself to feel the disappointment you may have over your circumstances. Your life plans may now be radically altered. Not only are you grieving for the loss of a normal child, you are grieving for what the disability means to your child, to you personally, and to your family's life as a whole. It's a lot to sort through at once. You don't have to maintain a "stiff upper lip" for anyone—not to protect your own spouse or parents, not to satisfy your minister or church members, and not to make the hospital staff or your pediatrician feel okay. If you don't allow yourself to experience your true feelings, if you repress them, they'll come out in some other manner, either physical, emotional, relational, or spiritual. Telling God you aren't very happy right now is all right—the omniscient One knows it anyway.

- For mothers especially—take care of yourself! You can't convey love and learning to your child when you are exhausted. Naps aren't ungodly; they're a gift from the Creator to allow us to restore our bodies. Learn to ask for what you need, from your spouse, your other children if they are of an age to help, your own parents and relatives, and your in-laws. Look at your household budget and decide how to fit in a housekeeper, even if you can only afford to hire a teenager to come in and do some basics. Using paper plates is perfectly acceptable when you have so many other important things to do. A microwave oven may be the only way hot meals will appear on your table. You can't afford not to make your life easier at this point because you need so much energy to care for your child.

- Prepare for the chaos hours of late afternoon and early evening, especially if you have more than one child. Everyone in the family is hungry and tired by this time of day, adults and children alike. Someone has to take responsibility for dinner, and the rule seems to be that children are hungry a half hour before dinner is ready but somehow not interested in eating when it's on the table. If parents are aware of the problems, they can take some steps to cooperate at the "worst" times of day and alleviate a major source of stress in their families.

- Learn to ask for what you need in medical care for your baby. When your baby has medical problems, you will have a lot of contact with doctors. Having a pediatrician who can act as a coordinator of information and services will be invaluable. With so many insurances in the form of HMOs (health maintenance organizations) or managed care, freedom of choice may be somewhat restricted, but it's important that you work within the range of options you have to obtain the person whom you feel will be best for you and the baby.

- Don't expect your pastor or minister to give you what he or she is unable to give. Clergy fulfill many roles. No one person can be expert in all areas. Ask your pastor for references for what you need, whether physical or emotional support and help. If what you want doesn't exist in your church, keep looking for a church that does have what you need. Sometimes it can be discouraging, and you can't get your specific needs met. In that case, you might have to go to a church council and state your needs and ask for a program to be started. You might be able to enlist the assistance of others who have the same needs. You might have to shorten your list of needs and compromise. Don't give up; sometimes things happen one small step at a time.

- From the beginning, cultivate a list of reliable baby-sitters and use them, whether they are from your church, teens from the neighborhood, or respite-care services. Chances are you will need all three types at some point. Set aside time for yourself, and get away as a couple. It's tempting to think that only you can take care of this little one who needs so much; but that will only make it easy for you to develop into an overprotective parent who will eventually never be away from this child, except when he or she is in school.

- Having a child with special needs can be an opportunity for growth unlike any you could have thought possible. You will have to draw on strengths you didn't know existed within you. You will bond with other parents who have children with special needs. The people in community programs and in schools that work with your children are special in themselves—exceptional individuals who have a particular brand of caring. As one parent said, "Normal seems so boring!" Faith takes on new dimensions daily with each new challenge. When Chris was born, I had no idea how this seven-pound baby would change how I viewed life and how I related to God.

8

YOUR CHILD AND SPECIAL EDUCATION

My first memory of seeing a disabled child in a school setting was when I was in the sixth grade. Because she had polio, Marianne used crutches and wore leg braces. I never saw Marianne after grade school, but I remember well that she was personable, bright, and fun to be with.

In college I took a course in "Exceptional Children." As part of that course, we had to visit six different schools, both public and private. One public-school setting was for children with physical disabilities, and one was for gifted children. The public schools did not accommodate most disabilities.

At that time, children with learning disabilities were ignored, called "slow learners," or treated as behavior problems. When I think back to the troublemakers who were either in grade school with me or in the classroom where I did my student teaching, I realize that their behavior stemmed

153

from unaddressed learning problems. Attention-deficit disorder (ADD) was not yet a diagnosis.

My college text for that course in exceptional children classified children with an IQ below seventy as either "idiots, imbeciles, or morons," depending on their test scores. Psychologists then looked at this group of children and screened out those who would not benefit from education. They were eliminated from the classroom.

The seventies brought about sweeping changes in education for children with special needs, in the form of the Education for All Handicapped Children Act of 1975, Public Law 94-142 (P.L. 94-142). Children who were previously excluded from a free, appropriate, public education were now to be included. The untiring efforts of thousands of parents birthed that law into existence. It not only opened public-school doors to many children with learning disabilities but also provided additional services to children already struggling in the classroom.

After almost fifteen years of having federally mandated special-education services (the law was implemented in 1977), schools are still wrestling with how best to provide education to all children. Special education covers a wide range of children, from the student who sees a speech therapist to correct a lisp, to a wheelchair-bound child who has neither speech nor normal capacities for sight and hearing—and all the possibilities in between.

I can't possibly begin to address all of the specifics about special education for your unique circumstances. No two school districts provide special education in the same manner; situations can vary even between two schools within the same district. I choose, therefore, to take a generalist approach and speak from my own experience, from what I have read and researched, and from the experiences of others I know.

PARENTAL RESPONSIBILITY
IN SPECIAL EDUCATION

You may feel that when your child enters school, you have taken a part-time job. To some degree your feelings are warranted. It's much more complex to have a child in special education than to have a child in "regular" education. One of the reasons for such complexity is that you will be part of the process of determining both placement and the Individualized Education Plan (IEP) for your child. When your child goes to school, your direct influence over what your child will learn ends at the school door. Parents, as voters and part of the community, can influence school curriculum, but in special education, you are asked to sign that you approve what the school has proposed to teach your child each year.

Having to sign the IEP puts on you a burden of responsibility. I used to feel pressure in a number of areas:

- Am I making the best decision for my child?
- I'm not a curriculum expert; I don't feel that I know what my options may be.
- What if this isn't the right choice? Will I carry some fault because I agreed to it?
- If I don't see to it that my child gets all that is needed now, in the school years, I may be very sorry later on.
- Who really knows what's right? How experienced is this teacher?
- Is the school trying to fit my child into one of its existing programs, or is it looking at my child's needs, and then designing a plan that will meet those needs?
- Where are the limits? How realistic am I being with what I would like to see happen? Did I give in too easily, or did I insist too much?

With the myriad of concerns that the IEP process alone can

raise, it's not a wonder that half of parents of children in special education do not attend IEP meetings. Some may not attend because of extraneous reasons, such as conflicts with work or unavailability of transportation. However, many schools make a decided effort to get parents to participate by providing evening hours for meetings and home visits. I suspect that parents don't participate in the IEP process for many unaddressed reasons:

- They may not feel up to the task of making wise choices.
- They may feel intimidated by the process or may have bad memories of school and not want to have anything to do with their child's school.
- They may resent that their child is in special education, or they may not agree with the particular placement in special education.
- They may be burned out and decide not to participate at this time.

On the other hand, parents may be relieved just to sign off on whatever the school wants and therefore have one less concern about their child.

PARENTAL ATTITUDES ABOUT SCHOOL

Your response to the educational aspect of your child's life may vary. You may feel that at this point it's not the highest priority. You may be heavily involved in other aspects of your child's development, such as medical issues, and therefore your interest in school might be lower. That's okay. If that's where you are finding yourself at this time, I encourage you to keep contact with the child's teacher, spell out how you will participate this school year, and convey your appreciation for what does happen at school. You don't have to explain the details of your life if you don't want to. If you basically agree with the Individualized Education Plan, go to the meeting or sign what is sent home, and let yourself off the hook.

If, however, you are harboring some bitterness toward the school or the teacher and if you don't participate because of your feelings about something that has happened in the past, I encourage you to rethink your strategy. No matter how you feel, your child does need school. You may not like the particular teacher assigned to your child, but sometimes nothing can be done to change that. Your noncooperative stance can harm your child, not because the teacher or school will be vindictive and take it out on the child, but because your input about your child is valuable to teachers.

In all fairness, teacher-training programs in colleges usually don't have courses in working with parents and families in a collaborative manner.[1] And teachers are not trained in all of the areas that relate to the child's disability. Their focus is on instruction. Over time, with seasoning and with maturity, teachers do gain expertise in many areas. Some teachers relate to parents very well. They have listening and empathizing skills that let you know that they understand you and value what you have to say. It is, however, unfair to expect teachers to be experts in all of the areas regarding your child; but you can show that you respect the knowledge and ability that they do have. You must have some kind of relationship with your child's teachers. For the sake of your child, make your relationship a friendly one at least.

Sometimes your dissatisfaction will be with the school system. It costs about twice as much to educate a child in special education as it does to provide regular education. Most children in special education are mainstreamed, which is the lowest-cost program available. Most children in special education are classified as learning disabled and speech impaired, and the vast majority of those children are in

157

regular classrooms, receiving either some therapy during the school day or attending a resource room for one or more periods.[2]

You may desire more services than the school offers, although, technically, services are supposed to fit the child and not vice versa. If your child is mainstreamed—that is, placed in a regular classroom for all or most of the day—you may or may not be satisfied, but often these decisions are made by administrators, not individual teachers.

It would be ideal, however, if you and your child's teachers could work in a collaborative manner for the child's benefit. Collaboration means that all of you are working toward common goals, that you share rights and responsibilities, and that you contribute jointly to the process. The marks of successful collaboration include

- mutual respect for skills and knowledge;
- honest and clear communication;
- shared, two-way information;
- mutual goals; and
- shared decision making and planning.[3]

Collaboration can occur when parents fully understand the process of evaluation and placement of their child. The tests your child is given will vary according to your school district; all will use some type of standardized testing as part of the evaluation process. When your child is tested, you have the right to have the test and its results explained to you fully. Some test reports will be given to you outright; others will be marked "confidential" but must be explained and interpreted to you because of their technical nature.

Special education involves more than academic instruction. The program for your child may consider other areas, such as self-help skills, occupational and physical therapy, socialization, and speech and language. Your child may need other services, such as catheterization, interpreters, or a braille typewriter. You may be concerned about accessibility of bathrooms, water fountains, and classrooms on the second floor, although, eventually, the Americans with Disabilities Act will cover these needs. You may be concerned about what happens on the school bus, that children in wheelchairs are facing forward and properly anchored at four points of attachment. Even if your child doesn't use a wheelchair, you may be concerned about the length of the ride, the availability of an aide, or the ability of the bus driver to radio or call for help if the bus becomes disabled.

A recent article about children who have asthma brought my attention to the fact that, although children need their inhalers immediately when they are having breathing difficulty, some schools require that all inhalers are kept in the school office, which restricts their availability in time of need. The article also pointed out that the incidence of asthma as well as the number of deaths of children due to asthma are on the rise in this country. This is a problem that schools will need to address.[4]

When we look at all of the varied issues regarding children with disabilities, it becomes clear that the demands on both teachers and parents are great and the potential for burnout is high.

INCLUDING YOUR CHILD IN THE IEP CONFERENCE

Another P.L. 94-142 stipulation that may cause a dilemma for you is that your child should attend the Individualized Education Plan conference if appropriate. The PACER Center (see page 246) offers the following advantages of including the child in the IEP meeting:

- The conference is more clearly focused on the child as an individual.
- The child has an opportunity to learn self-advocacy.
- The child learns the following life skills:
  —goal setting,
  —understanding of his or her own learning,
  —strengths and needs,
  —expression of his or her own needs and concerns,
  —the process of resolving differences.[5]

You may not want to bring your child to the IEP meeting for a variety of reasons: you feel your child is too young; it's a new idea and you don't know how to proceed; the child doesn't want to attend; you feel the meetings are stressful for the child; or you tried it once and it didn't work. The Pacer Center offers some suggestions that may help in including the child in the IEP conference.

- Sit down with your child and talk over the year's learning goals. Explain what each goal means in language the child understands.
- Discuss with your child how it would feel to attend a parent conference. Would the child like to attend? Would the child be willing to share some ideas or thoughts? How would the child react if someone said something that the child felt was negative?
- Stage a role play of the conference to help the child phrase exactly what he or she would like to say.
- Consider having your child present for only part of the conference, if that seems more comfortable.
- If your child attends a conference and it isn't successful, rethink what happened. Ask the child what might have been done differently. Don't give up because one incident didn't go well.

SPECIAL-EDUCATION SUCCESS STORIES

Although you may feel frustrated with the school system at times, remember that a lot of good things happen to your child at school. School provides your child with the opportunity for experiences unavailable elsewhere. I could generate a long list of the benefits that Chris gained from school—from the curriculum as well as from the many caring people who taught him over the years.

With integration of special-education programs into regular school buildings in our city has come recognition of talents of students in special education. A school-board newsletter carried a picture of the mayor giving awards for outstanding students in special education: Vachelle, a teenager who has no vision, is a drummer with local jazz groups and attends the Governor's Magnet School for the Arts; Ian, an eleven-year-old with Down Syndrome, was on the U.S. Olympic Swim Team and is his school's official photographer. A local paper published a story about Vince, an eleven-year-old in special education who, with the help of a peer, has the job of filling the soda machine at school. The story described that school's unique peer program where children in regular education act as friends and aides to students in special education.

First-grader Casey, born without a right tibia, ankle, and knee, required amputation of the limb and adjustment to a prosthesis. With the help of a counselor, Casey and her mother took to class a model of her leg and some dolls to demonstrate to her classmates what would happen to her. Not only did Casey's self-esteem enjoy a boost from having such a unique show-and-tell presentation, but her classmates understood more about her and subsequently other people with disabilities.[6] I've read other stories of parents going into classrooms with their children to explain the nature of the child's disability or some pending medical treatment, helping the other students to have knowledge and understanding.

PARENTS AS MOTIVATORS
OF THEIR CHILDREN

You are often the key in developing motivation in your special-needs child. All talent needs fostering and encouragement because talent alone is not enough: practice and persistence are required for mastery. Most children with special needs need extra motivation to learn subject matter, self-help skills, and behavior control.

You can help motivate your child. You may have to change your expectations of your child; you may set your standards too high or too low. It's fine to expect success from your child, but you may have to redefine what success means.

I learned a lesson in motivation the year I decided to have Chris learn to fix his own sandwiches for summer day camp. I assembled the ingredients for him, but I soon learned that I had to teach Chris several lessons before he could actually make the sandwich, which was the relatively easy part. Chris had to learn how to open a stubborn peanut butter jar. Next, he had to deal with the twisty-tie on the end of the loaf of bread, both opening it and closing it. After we got to the actual sandwich making, he had to learn to wrap the sandwich properly and not to put it on the bottom of the lunch bag before putting in other items that would crush it.

If I had stopped with, "He can't open jars so he'll never get to making his own lunch," I would not have given him a chance for success. He didn't learn to pack a lunch the first time—or for the first few weeks of trying. But he did learn other things in small steps that led to success.

REALISTIC EXPECTATIONS

To motivate your children to learn, you need to keep in mind that your expectations must be realistic. If you have unrealistic expectations, you create failure; if you have conflicting expectations, you set up confusion. If your child lacks interest in learning a new skill or in controlling certain behavior, maybe your child hasn't developed a sense of curiosity or the child remembers past failures and doesn't want to try. Your child may also fear the unknown or may expect to fail. Or your child may fear being criticized, punished, rejected, or appearing different if he or she takes a risk to try new behavior.

In the movie *What About Bob,* the psychiatrist father is trying to teach his son to dive. The child senses that he can't meet his dad's expectations of a perfect performance, and he develops a fear of diving. Every day he tries, and every day he fails. And every day the father sees his son as a failure. Finally one day the child's dive is successful, much to his surprise. At that moment, the father rushes in to "take over" and give more instructions, to establish that he, the parent, is clearly in charge.

Your goal as a parent is to build, not tear down. Motivate your child in these important areas:

- Guide your child through the process in small steps: demonstrate each step, encourage the child to attempt each step, and then specifically praise what was accomplished at each step.
- Reward your child for participation and accomplishment. Chose a reward that your child values, and use rewards in moderation so that your child doesn't feel devalued by over-rewarding.
- Stimulate your child to be interested in the unknown or

in areas of past failures. *Suggest* is the key word here. Introduce a new subject, or provide an opportunity to try something in an atmosphere of fun or perhaps even intrigue.

- Let go of your own agenda and allow your child to explore on his or her own. Your child needs free time, so encourage independent activity. Provide the materials and then back off, not judging what results, but allowing the activity to be the child's domain.

Be careful not to overstimulate your child, especially if your child has a learning disability like ADD (attention-deficit disorder) or ADHD (attention-deficit-hyperactivity disorder) or emotional problems with or without other disabilities. Overstimulation can hinder the child from coping adequately.

CHANGING CHILDREN'S BEHAVIOR

Sometimes you may feel that you are spending so much time disciplining and regulating your child's behavior that you don't have time to be a motivator. You often get caught up in automatic patterns of dealing with your child. For example, you ask your child to do something, and the child doesn't comply; you then remind your child, and the child still doesn't comply. So you punish. I've not added the shouting and emotional content that often accompanies such an interchange.

A suggested technique for breaking this cycle is "Stop! Look! Listen!"[7] Before you slip into the usual mode when your child is disobedient, *stop*. Then *look* at what your child is doing and *listen* to what your child is saying before you jump in to ask questions, criticize, or punish. "Stop! Look! Listen!" slows down your automatic process and therefore decreases the likelihood of an escalation of emotions. It also stops the child from slipping into the usual modes of resistance. When you treat your child in a different way, that child will respond to you differently also.

If you want to change your child's behavior, keep these basic principles in mind.

- Encourage your child to be responsible for his or her own behavior, to gain self-control.
- Be honest, open, and supportive to your child so that you establish an atmosphere of mutual respect.
- Determine what happens immediately before and after your child does something you find undesirable. You may be able to change circumstances so that the events that set off the behavior do not occur. You may also be able to change what happens after the behavior so that the child doesn't gain undeserved attention for negative behavior.
- Clearly explain to the child the consequences for undesirable behavior. Be clear about the behaviors you do expect.
- Establish logical consequences for behavior. Spanking a child for hitting reinforces that hitting works. Use a "time out" or other objective consequence. Be consistent in using consequences.
- "Catch" the child doing desired behavior and reward it. You may have to use tangible rewards at first, such as snacks, but intersperse those with hugs, smiles, compliments.
- Always let the child know why you are giving positive reinforcement. For effective learning to occur, the child must know what behavior prompted your reinforcement.
- Don't try to change too much at one time. Target one behavior and work on it. Inform the teacher of what you

are doing at home, and try to establish a consistency in the goals your child is working on in school and the goals your child is working on at home.[8]

BE A SUPPORTIVE PARENT

Many models of parenting have been offered throughout the years. One model that has value to parents of children with special needs is that of the supportive parent, a model developed to help parents whose children are in Special Olympics. Many qualities of the supportive parent are easily transferred to the school setting. The supportive parent:

- Focuses on mastery and strategy rather than competitive ranking. The performance that the child can control is productive, while concentrating on winning or losing is not.
- Makes the child feel valuable no matter what the outcome.
- Believes that experiences provide self-development opportunity. Lifelong values are what is really important.
- Understands that the child is taking risks, but giving one's best is what counts.
- Communicates true concerns with coaches (teachers).
- Understands the difference between parental role and coach (teacher) role.
- Thinks positively, even when the child has not performed well.
- Doesn't use fear and punishment to pressure the child to improve performance.
- Avoids criticizing and reminding the child what he or she needs to do better.
- Gives needed emotional support.

166

- Recognizes and understands behaviors that indicate the child feels insecure.
- Doesn't use guilt to manipulate the child.
- Allows the child to express what he or she is feeling and gives an empathic response: "Yes, I know that you're worried about who your new teacher will be. Let me help you get ready for school."[9]

SHOULD MY CHILD BE IN A CHRISTIAN SCHOOL?

You may find yourself in a dilemma of wanting to provide a Christian education for your child, either in Christian schools or by home schooling, but because your child has special needs, your only recourse may be public education. You may be able to home school your child up to a certain point. You may have the finances to afford Christian education, but the school may not be equipped to provide what your child needs. Some Christian schools do have some components of special education, but often those components cost parents additional funds. As a parent of a child with special needs, you constantly need to rethink your beliefs, including your stance on education.

Avoid getting caught up in the doctrine or policy of a particular church. Keep in mind that your child is only on loan to you, that he or she really belongs to Christ. Jesus said to parents, "Let the little children come to me" (Matt. 19:14). What does it mean to let your child go to Jesus? Would public education help or hinder your child's process of going to Jesus? If the services help the child learn, develop a positive self-concept, and understand himself or herself and the world we live in, then the public education may be a vehicle to Jesus.

When a child has needs met, learning about Jesus is more likely to take place.

A child can also learn to appreciate all the people Jesus provides to show that child how much he loves him or her. People who teach your child to read, to care for himself or herself, and to manage life reflect God's care, whether or not those people are Christians. God shows his love to us through many people, not only those who belong to a church.

As a Christian parent, you also may have a ministry in public settings. Your steadfastness of faith, your caring of your child, and your interactions with school personnel are your living witness of God's working in your life. You may never be aware of leading someone in the school to Christ, but you may, by the way you live your life, inspire others to seek out what gives you strength and peace. You may be the only Gospel your neighbors ever read.

You are the one to make the decision about what is best for your child, and you are responsible to God for that decision. The religious beliefs of your child's teachers may not be as important as your own willingness to follow God's leading for your child.

9

LIVING AWAY
FROM HOME

Most parents expect their children to leave home eventually; leaving is a natural event in the family life cycle. However, children with special needs often don't fit normal expectations. And the decision about where your child will live at various stages of his or her life is difficult to make.

Before the 1970s, children with disabilities were either institutionalized or kept at home without benefit of education. After the concepts of normalization and deinstitutionalization became prevalent and with the passage of P.L. 94-142, children with special needs were kept in the family home and educated in local schools. Over the past twenty years trends turned almost completely around. In researching ten years of past editions of *Exceptional Parent* magazine, I found only five articles about residential placement of children.

The ideal would seem to be that your children would continue to live with your family. However, not all families are equipped to meet the special needs of their children. If we lived in a perfect world, outside services would support all families who wanted to keep their children at home. Adequate home health care, respite services, tutoring, behavioral management, specialized equipment, recreation, vocational training, transportation, and finances would be provided. The real-world situation, however, is that at the same time that medical technology saves more special-needs babies, the public funding to provide services to those children is declining every year.

The family has also changed in the last decade. Families in which both parents work or in which a single parent is the only income provider have increasing need of community services to care for their children in the home. Community agencies are unable to keep up with family needs in current times.

OUR EXPERIENCE WITH RESIDENTIAL PROGRAMS

Twice Chris's father and I made the decision for Chris to live away from home. Both decisions were difficult, and neither was made hastily. The first time Chris was seven years old; the second time he was twenty-two. They were two separate decisions, based on separate circumstances that reflected the stage of the whole family at the time as much as Chris's particular needs.

PLACING CHRIS AT AGE SEVEN

When Chris was seven years old, Jim and I decided that residential placement was necessary—as much for us as it was for him. Many factors contributed to our decision. The first was that Jim was in the military and gone from home a good deal. We had two other children at the time, one older than Chris and one younger. Chris's behavior was unmanageable and did not show hope of improvement. I told the story of the golf counter earlier, illustrating the lack of services to help parents at that time. I was working with a Navy pediatrician who was interested in Chris and provided something that I hadn't experienced before in the military—an ongoing relationship with one doctor over a long period of time. My level of distress was such that when he recommended three books to me, I didn't have the energy to call a bookstore and place orders for them. I had an immediate need for help, and waiting for books to arrive seemed hopeless. I know that his intentions were good, but his inability to provide referrals that would have been of immediate assistance is further evidence of inadequate services. This doctor directed our search for residential placement and gave us options for choice of placement.

A second factor was lack of suitable programs that would have allowed Chris to stay at home. This was before P.L. 94-142, and the local schools didn't have classes appropriate for Chris. He was attending classes in a local private school for children with disabilities, but it was unable to provide what he needed. The school was apparently short on funding but long on need.

The third factor was financial. Because Chris's father was in the military, we had some options for financing residential services through CHAMPUS (military medical insurance for dependents and retirees). In addition to that, the local school system would provide some funding.

We were faced with a number of limitations in our search. One was geographic. We wanted to keep the distance within a day's drive. The other, and most important, was program;

Chris needed a program that would be structured enough to teach him self-help skills and flexible enough to provide opportunities for enjoyment and pursuit of an individual learning program. We also had to stay within CHAMPUS regulations, and the cost had to be affordable.

We consulted with the pediatrician and decided to pay a visit to the Devereaux School in Pennsylvania, a six-hour drive from our home. We arranged for Chris to be evaluated by staff on the day that we were visiting. The setting and the grounds were beautiful—lots of trees and grass, rolling hills, attractive buildings. The residential cottage for Chris's age group was inviting, with bedrooms that two children shared, a common kitchen, and a living room for games and gathering. Everything was pleasing and as home-like as possible. The dining hall, gym, and swimming pool were all adjacent to the cottage, as were school rooms and medical-care facilities. We met most of the staff and learned the daily and weekend routine and were satisfied that Chris would be well cared for. In adding up the factors that led to the decision for residential placement, the first qualification was the quality of care. All that we saw led us to believe that he would benefit from the Devereaux School.

Over the two years that Chris lived away from home, he made progress. He learned a number of self-help skills that gave him more assurance about himself. Although it was slow going, he learned socialization skills, such as sharing of toys, one of the areas that was of such difficulty at home. I remember my excitement at seeing the small gains he had made. On one visit we took him out to lunch, and he drank his beverage through a straw, something we were unable to teach him! Jim and I looked at him and each other in amazement. He was not aware that he was doing anything out of the ordinary.

I had mixed feelings about placing Chris in a residential school. On the one hand, it gave me freedom from the constant caregiving, freedom from the behaviors that we were unable to control, and freedom to have somewhat of a normal experience of raising children. On the other hand, I was frustrated because I couldn't explain to Chris why he was being sent to school; his comprehension was at the level of a two- or three-year-old. It was difficult not to be with him on his birthday or on Thanksgiving. I would send him packages once a month, but I always had a hard time trying to decide what to send him. Then I had to box, wrap, and ship the package, and start the process again for the next month's package.

Occasionally we would take the other children and visit him for a weekend. This was a difficult process, as I recall. It was hard for our other children to be confined within a motel room. We would have to find suitable activities that they could enjoy together, not always easy in an unfamiliar town. Also, if Chris needed shoes or a bathing suit or other items, we would shop for those, again, in places that were unfamiliar. An underlying consideration was the expense of the trip itself, for gas, lodging, and meals.

After Chris was enrolled at the Devereaux School, my husband and I were surprised by the discovery that I was again pregnant. This pregnancy, unlike the others, was not easy. I was hospitalized twice and had to restrict my activities for the final three months. When our son Shawn was born, he remained in the hospital for a week but was fine after that. Throughout all of this, I don't know how I could have managed had Chris been at home. As I try to recall past events and my thoughts and feelings at the time, I wonder if the residential placement was God's provision for giving me some space to have this fourth child. I suppose I won't know until I get to heaven (I have a very long list of questions to ask when I get there!).

Chris came home three times a year, for two weeks each time—Christmas, spring, and summer. When Chris would arrive home for a stay, I was eager to check through his clothes and see what needed to be mended or replaced. It was tangible evidence that I was continuing to be a mother to him, when mothering was done by others most of the time.

Chris's stay at Devereaux ended when tuition increased dramatically, and we couldn't afford the extra thousands of dollars that were required. Also because P.L. 94-142 was starting implementation, the local public school finally had programs that would benefit Chris.

PLACING CHRIS AT AGE TWENTY-TWO

The second time we made the decision to place Chris in a residential facility, we made the decision for totally different reasons. I also found the second decision much harder than the first. Over the years I had become very close to Chris, and having him live away was like sending part of myself away. His ability to understand living away from home had not increased much, and I felt the same mixed feelings as the first time. Chris had a year to prepare for moving away from home. He visited the new residence with his school class. His teachers discussed it with him throughout the year, but I don't think he was able fully to comprehend what it meant.

I would call him weekly, and at first his conversations on the phone were limited to one-word replies to my questions or comments. The first time he asked, "Take me home?" my heart went to my shoe. I wanted to get in the car and pick him up that night. It was no easier on the weekends that he would come home for a visit and say, all the way back, "I want to stay home."

In one sense, Chris is in residential placement because of lack of community services. As a single parent, I can't keep a job and also keep Chris at home. If respite care was available as needed, if our community had vocational opportunities with transportation, if he had recreational outlets and opportunities to be with friends—then his living at home might be feasible. He can't care for himself while I'm away at work, but he would also be miserable living with me, as he needs work and friends, just as we all do. Living at home, even with employment, would leave him isolated from peers. When he does come home on weekends or vacations, I expend a great deal of effort to keep him entertained and busy.

Even though the decision for placement this second time was made with a great deal of thought, planning, and prayer, the letting go was not easy. I told the story in my first book of how I spent a day sewing labels on his clothes and crying. Other moms have had similar feelings. Carol Moczygemba wrote, "During those months of preparation, I found little time to dwell on what might lie ahead. There was so much to be done. But in the quiet times, when I was alone and packing the books, photos, and countless reminders of the good times spent with Stephanie, with family and friends, I would freeze with doubt and fear." Carol decided to place her daughter at age thirteen, a decision that has been successful. She always wonders if she did the right thing: "Like so many other parents who make momentous and difficult decisions for their children, I take solace where I find it and go on with life."[1]

Chris has progressed on his road to independence through all the experiences of his life, whether he was with his family or away. One weekend, when my seventeen-year-old son and a friend took Chris out to lunch and then came back and told me what a nice time they had with him, I realized that perhaps we can better appreciate the gift Chris is when we get some distance and are not his constant caregivers.

Chris's social skills have improved by great leaps in the last three years. He has had to interact with a wide variety of people—both peers and staff—in different situations, and the experience has been beneficial. I will not be here forever for him, and I'm grateful for what he can learn from others to become as independent as possible.

Placement is never an easy decision. The first time I don't think it occurred to me to pray about the circumstances; I believe that I was in such distress that God just took over for me, led me, and guided me through the hazy clouds of my confusion. The second time I put a lot of prayer into the decision. I was more rational and in control, and I made a choice based on logic. However, both decisions were equally difficult emotionally, and each brought challenges to our family.

I tell my story to share insights about residential placement, although my story isn't yet over. Chris is ending his allotted four years at his current placement, and by the time this book is published, he will probably be in a new situation. I believe that God knows where that place is and is already preparing it for him. I'm doing my homework, investigating possibilities, and praying about the situation. This time the decision is not *if* to place Chris, but *where* to place him. I recognize that it's not feasible for Chris to live with me. I enjoy our times together, but he needs more than I can give. He is entitled to a full life, and his life with me would be limited, subject to what I could do for him within the confines of my work.

I realize that each parent and child has an individual story of circumstances. I would not begin to presume that my situation applies to everyone. As I thought about offering some general guidelines for placement, I felt inadequate to the task. However, the following comments may help you formulate your own plan for what is best for your child.

WHEN TO PLACE

Obviously no one rule covers all aspects of when to place a child in a residential school. This is a highly individual decision. You must consider the needs of the child with the disability as well as the needs of your family as a whole. Sometimes people outside of the family can clearly see the benefits of placing the child in a residence, but because caring for the child meets parental needs, the child stays at home. In that case, the decision not to place sacrifices the welfare of the child to meet the needs of the parents.

Parents may not be able to place a child because they see it as a sign of failure, and they feel guilty for not being able to care for the child themselves. They play the martyrs and feel they are self-sacrificing; but this motive is not scripturally based. We are told to love others as we love ourselves. Loving the child means doing what is best for the child and then taking adult responsibility for dealing with our own insecurities and guilt feelings.

Parents should consider placement not as a failure but as an opportunity for the child to grow and develop. Placement is a solution to a problem, a means of coping with a difficult situation. It can be God's will and provision for your child and your family.

Some parents may measure their worth as persons by how they provide for their children. If all of a parent's worth is in childcare, then placement may bring about the empty-nest problems that emerge when one's children are grown. The empty-nest syndrome usually affects middle-aged women and their midlife roles. However, parents who place their child, especially one who has required intense caregiving, also experience the empty-nest syndrome. Research has shown that women who have other roles in life besides mothering make the most successful adjustment to the empty nest.[2]

Placing a child in a residential setting affords opportunities to develop other roles in life. If both parents are in the family, usually the father will already have a work role. He may now be free to develop leisure and hobby interests, expanding his roles. If the mother was not already working outside the home, she may be able to pursue vocational, educational, or leisure interests that were unattainable because of care of the child. In addition, the couple may find more time for each other and their other children.

EXPLORING PLACEMENT OPTIONS

Other elements in the decision to place a child in a residential school center on some of the concerns I mentioned regarding Chris.

- Where can your child best be served? What kind of a program will best meet your child's needs?
- What family circumstances lead you to believe that residential placement is the answer?
- Are there any community services that will enable you to keep your child at home?
- What limits have you found on placement (waiting lists, finances, distance)?
- What will be the positive and negative aspects of this placement? Will the positive outweigh the negative?

178

LOOKING FOR THE RIGHT PLACE

You can never have too much information about a possible placement for your child. Time spent in research will be of inestimable value later on. The more you know, the more you will have peace of mind when you make a decision. Both parents should be involved in this information-gathering process. One should not have the responsibility for doing the research and then presenting it to the other. Both should be fully involved in the decision process so that if the choice is not a fully satisfactory one, both parents accept the consequences rather than one parent blaming the other.

Some resources to explore for information include

- your pediatrician;
- a children's hospital;
- the local mental-retardation/mental-health agency;
- the Yellow Pages of the phone book for disability-related organizations;
- a local computerized information center;
- Yellow Pages of other cities (the reference librarian will be able to help you to find these on microfiche) to look for lists of schools;
- your school district's special-education office;
- the state licensing departments, which have lists of all licensed facilities in that state;
- professional journals, such as *American Journal of Mental Retardation*, and *The Journal of Learning Disabilities*, available in university libraries;
- a local or state parent organization, such as one of the parent-to-parent programs, or the Association for Retarded Citizens or a federally sponsored parent center, such as PACER in Minneapolis or PEATC in Alexandria, Virginia;

179

- professional organizations, such as the American Association of Mental Retardation or the Council for Exceptional Children. These organizations often have conferences that are open to parents as well as professionals.
Parents are usually given a special discount on the cost of
the conference. At the AAMR conference I learned of
many residential services, both private and public,
throughout the country. Ask your child's teachers what
professional organization they join, or call a university
special-education department for names of professional
organizations.

TYPES OF PLACEMENTS AVAILABLE

You must be aware of the specific type of setting you need.
Most organizations will specify that they are a school that
offers programs for specific disabilities. The following list
explains some of the abbreviations you may encounter:

- CCI—Child Care Institution (for any child with physi-
cal/mental disabilities, age eighteen and under).
- CRA—Community Residential Alternative (for any age
of child or adult, with any mental/physical disability that
requires twenty-four-hour supervision, with a maximum
capacity of eight persons).
- SNF—Skilled Nursing Facility (generally the same
concept as the CRA, but for more medically involved
people requiring specialized medical care).
- CLF—Community Living Facility (Moderate care to
light supervision is offered for those with mild-to-moderate mental retardation/developmental disabilities, age
eighteen and older).
- ICF—Intermediate Care Facility (also called ICFDD;

for those who have developmental disabilities that require some nursing care, age eighteen and older).

- SLA—Supported Living Arrangement (generally a residence in an apartment or townhouse for those with mild-to-moderate disabilities that require light supervision, age eighteen and older).
- HIP—Home Intervention Program (similar to foster care, where one or two people with disabilities live with a family in a single home, age eighteen and older).[3]

Your own community may have programs similar to these but with slightly different titles. Generally, the description will fit one of these categories.

You may discover that you have another option to a residential school. It may be possible for your child to live in a community residential alternative (CRA) or skilled nursing facility (SNF) in your own community and attend the local school. It is helpful to keep options open when you are exploring possibilities. I find that when I'm locked on to a particular solution for a problem, I may miss better options along the way.

MAKING A SITE VISIT

When you visit a possible residence for your child, go with a notebook listing your questions, with space under each to allow you to jot in answers. Use other pages for lists, such as names and positions of staff, organizational structure (who reports to whom), financial information, and any other information that may be pertinent to your child. As soon as possible after the visit, sit down and write out your general impressions, feelings, and unanswered questions. If you allow time to pass before doing this, you may forget details that would be helpful later on in making your decision.

You may also want to bring a camera for pictures of the grounds and individual rooms. If you decide to enroll your child, the pictures will be helpful in preparing the child for what is ahead. Taking pictures of your child in the setting will be another way of preparing your child.

Make the site visit with another person, either a spouse or a trusted friend. Agree beforehand to look for certain qualities. Then compare your observations and perceptions afterward.

Make a list of issues that are crucial to your decision. If you enjoy systematic approaches to decision making, you can list each factor that you consider necessary and give it a weight of from one to ten. For example, "close to home" might be a +5 factor for you, while "indoor swimming pool" may be only a +1. If you are comparing two or more places, you might use your system in comparisons.

The quality of the staff is a crucial factor in determining the adequacy of a facility. Of course, you will want to ascertain that the facility is properly licensed, but licensing does not define the quality of caring.

First, determine the level of staff training, especially for those people who will provide psychological assessment, medical care, and special-education classes. Second, assess the quality of loving care shown to residents. You are, in effect, placing your child with surrogate parents. You want to be sure that your child will be cared for with love. Love does cover a multitude of sins and is a prime ingredient in successful programs. My faith is constantly reaffirmed by the quality of people who work in residential settings for children and adults with disabilities. I am aware of cases of abuse, also, but those are not the norm. Most workers are dedicated, giving, caring people, and some see their work as ministry, not just employment.

182

LIVING AWAY FROM HOME—A GRADUAL PROCESS

If possible, make the transition to a residential setting a gradual one. Begin by using respite services for a day or an evening so that your child gets used to being with other caregivers. Or take a vacation for a weekend, week, or longer and have your child cared for in your home or at a respite-care center. Or send your child to a residential summer camp. *Exceptional Parent* magazine has an annual camp directory that lists camps for children with special needs. You might start the child with a one-week experience and expand it.

When you have made a decision about a certain place, first allow your child to stay for a trial week or two. This will be somewhat artificial, but, especially if the child can comprehend that this is only for a week, it may be a valuable prelude to the longer stay. In some places, parents may be able to stay in guest quarters during the trial visit. If so, take advantage of the opportunity. Try to see both a weekday and a Saturday or Sunday so you get a feel for the differences and similarities between week and weekend routines. Eat meals with residents if you can.

If your child does well, then when the time for placement comes, he or she will be going back to a place with good memories. If it's not a good experience, you will benefit by finding out from the staff specifically what didn't go well. It may be that certain changes need to be made to accommodate your child, and you might want to try another week after the changes are made. You may discover that this is not the place for your child. Then continue your search.

PREVENT PLACEMENT IN CRISIS SITUATIONS

Another factor in placing a child is timing. When I placed Chris almost twenty years ago, I had no idea that another baby was coming. But if I had known, I would have made sure that the placement occurred long before the baby's arrival. It would have been very hard for the new baby to arrive and then for Chris to leave immediately. The message to him would have been that he was being replaced.

If you periodically discuss your child's progress and future, you probably will avoid a crisis placement. Keep your will current, giving specific instructions for what you wish to happen to all of your children if both parents should die. Although it's rare for both parents to die at one time, it does happen. The last thing you would want is for the courts to decide where your child would be placed.

I have included in the Appendix a list from my previous book on what to ask before placing your child. The questions grew out of my own experience, and you may find them helpful in your planning.

Your own prayer life and faith are components in this process. Before I had a faith walk that was Christ-centered and part of my everyday life (as opposed to my previous Sunday-only and sometimes-foxhole faith), I didn't have a peace about where Chris was going to be living as he became older. The difference now is that although I still have to do investigating, weighing, and interviewing, I have a peace about the process. I know that God's hand is in all of this, and that even if situations are not seemingly optimal at the time, everything will work out. I don't mean that in a Pollyanna sense; I mean it in a sense of trust in a Creator who is the source of all providence and provision.

AFTER PLACEMENT

Once you have placed your child, the process doesn't end. Rather, a shift of focus occurs, and you begin a new phase. You must now be aware of some new concepts:

- First, if your child is young, you may be involved in several placements in the future. If your child is in school now, he or she most likely will go to an adult residence after age twenty-two.

- Second, even after your child is in an adult residence, you may need to change the child's residence. The first placement may not work out, or things at the setting may change. Don't blame yourself or feel that you missed God's leading. Some things are for a season only, and we may never know why things changed. Take the skills that you have learned about decision making and begin working on the next decision.

- Third, be prepared for a hole in your life. You will have free time that may feel strange. You may be so used to being programmed for care of the child that the idea of time for yourself never occurred to you. The thought that you are free to choose what you want to do with your time may be so foreign that it produces anxiety. This is normal for a new situation.

- Also, be prepared for having mixed feelings of relief that you are free from care and of guilt for not being "good enough" to care for your child yourself. Take these to God, thanking and praising and trusting that this is for the child's good. The child, after all, is only on loan to you and ultimately belongs to the Father.

- Develop a thick skin when around others who may unknowingly make comments that may sound hurtful to you. People have said to me, "I wouldn't mind taking care of him all the time. He's a lot of fun." "He goes

185

everywhere with me with no problem, always a gentle-man." "He's such a neat kid and nice to be around." While people may just be trying to make you feel good, keep in mind that they have no idea what twenty-four hours a day, every day, are like, and they also have no idea of the child's many needs.

- Be aware that you may "romanticize" what having the child at home was like. We have selective memory, and you may find yourself saying that it wasn't so hard and question why you did this. This may especially be true if you have a strong identity with the child. You may feel that part of you is gone, that you are incomplete. Take this also to God, and ask what God has for you now.

You can find many ways to use the energy that you formerly put into your child, and this gift of time can be spent in good stewardship. God may give you some specific work, or he may be encouraging you to take some time to care for yourself, to enjoy your family and your surroundings. Whatever the situation, open yourself to the Holy Spirit's leading and don't spend time berating yourself.

"There is a time for everything, and a season for every activity under heaven" (Eccl. 3:1). Your calendar may be divided into four seasons, but your life has many seasons. And in each season you are called to experience, to feel, and to grow in your Christian life. In some seasons you may be joyful, in others sad, in some peaceful, and in some troubled. Parents of children with special needs know about these seasons and how much their own experience of them is bound to what is happening with their child. Even though your child may live away from home, the invisible cords, of sheerest silk though they may be, are still there. Placing your child outside of your home is not abandonment; it's giving opportunity for the child, you, and your family to experience this season of your life in a new way and to grow together in God's love.

10

ADVOCATING FOR YOUR CHILD

One September day, when Christopher was a teenager and a new school year had begun, I was reflecting on what had happened over the past several school years. I thought about all of the IEP meetings at which I would present my case to teachers and administrators about what I felt Chris needed from school and the negotiations that would subsequently occur. I was thinking not so much about the content of the meetings but the process that occurred over the years. When I became the parent of a child with a disability, I unknowingly took on a role that came as a surprise—the role of an advocate.

According to the dictionary, an advocate is one who pleads the cause of another.[1] Without realizing exactly what had taken place through the years, I had become Chris's advocate, a role I will need to fill for the rest of my life.

As a parent, I was prepared for certain duties and

obligations inherent in caring for children: speaking for them when they're too young to do so for themselves; intervening in situations that they can't handle; supporting them until they're ready to leave home.

But the advocacy role I had grown into was almost a public function. I would have to interact across a broad spectrum of organizations and individuals for Chris. Parenting had a new slant. It was as if I didn't have a choice; Chris's situation required it of me. Advocating for Chris was very different from advocating for our other children, whose basic human rights were rarely, if ever, in question. With Chris's situation, I had to be vigilant to see that his rights were not overlooked, that he would receive services to which he was entitled, and that he was treated fairly and with equity.

I found definite disparities between how special-needs students and regular students were treated. For instance, I never had to advocate for the right of the other children to be taught to read, but I had to press to make sure Chris had that same opportunity. Students without disabilities are given a choice about which vocational areas to study; students with disabilities may be tested, but the courses they are offered are not so much a reflection of what they need but of what the school offers. The criteria are not always fair to the student. In one situation, Chris was said to be not suitable for a vocational program because he hadn't learned the skill of getting his lunch alone and reporting to another building on time. However, no one even considered teaching him those skills so that he could get to the training program on time. As a result, he was eliminated from the program.

Advocacy for children with special needs doesn't end when children are no longer in school. It will continue throughout their lifetimes as they need housing, jobs, recreation, medical and dental care, and other services. When the parents are no longer alive or able to be advocates, others, whether family members or agency workers, will have to take up the role.

SCRIPTURAL BASIS FOR ADVOCACY

Advocacy is usually spoken of in human services, but strangely it isn't often spoken of in the church. As I researched synonyms for the words *advocate* and *advocacy,* I became aware of the basic Christian principles in these words. Advocacy is what God the Father, Jesus the Son, and the Holy Spirit do for us. Synonyms for *advocacy* are "support, backing, patronage, active espousal, maintenance, sustenance." Synonyms for *advocate* are "maintainer, sustainer, upholder, supporter, backer, patron, promoter, endorser, favorer, defender, champion, vindicator, pleader, activist, intercessor, interceder, mediator, paraclete."[2]

As I reflected on these words, the words of Scripture came to mind:

- "But because Jesus lives forever, he has a permanent priesthood. Therefore he is able to save completely those who come to God through him, because he always lives to intercede for them" (Heb. 7:24–25).
- "In the same way, the Spirit helps us in our weakness. We do not know what we ought to pray for, but the Spirit himself intercedes for us with groans that words cannot express. And he who searches our hearts knows the mind of the Spirit, because the Spirit intercedes for the saints in accordance with God's will" (Rom. 8:26–27).
- "Christ Jesus, who died—more than that, who was raised to life—is at the right hand of God and is also interceding for us" (Rom. 8:34).

I'm able to take comfort in the fact that as I intercede for

189

my child, Jesus and the Holy Spirit intercede for me. When I become tired of this role of advocate, I am sustained by remembering that I have advocates who are sustaining me. I can, in faith, take things one step further and believe that God goes before me to advocate and prepare the way with others. Recently I was preparing for a meeting about Chris, and I felt as if my past pleas had fallen on deaf ears. In prayer I told God how tired I was of the ongoing situation, and that I didn't want to be the initiator of my proposal again. When I got to the meeting, I could barely believe my ears. The people in charge of the program said that they had been considering the circumstances and they had decided that it was time for a change—and the change was exactly what I had hoped to see happen.

Sometimes I've had to be persistent, like the widow who kept demanding justice of the judge in Luke 18. I'm sure that in some cases people may have thought toward me as that judge did of the widow, "Even though I don't fear God or care about men, yet because this widow keeps bothering me, I will see that she gets justice, so that she won't eventually wear me out with her coming!" (Luke 18:4). In those times, God often puts people in my path to encourage me to persevere, to give me information I need, or just to support me.

What do we hope to gain for our children by advocating for them? Some of the concepts in the Scripture passages offer direction: We want our child's interests kept before those who provide programs and services. We want our child's service providers to have the child's best interest in mind. We want our child not to be forgotten. We want these things now and especially later, when we are no longer able to be a spokesperson for our child.

As we advocate for our child, we provide a powerful model for others to follow. Other family members can learn from our example how to help the special-needs child. Even the child may learn the important lessons of advocacy so that as the child grows into adulthood, he or she can learn self-advocacy.

THE CHILDREN'S CREED

The following "Children's Creed" provides a framework for what we would hope to attain for our children. It was written with all children in mind, not just those with special needs. In order to grow, each child deserves

- love, honor, and freedom from stigma throughout life;
- the celebration of being special;
- a life-sharing family, home, and nurturing adult support;
- a community of concern and friendships;
- economic security, health, and the full benefits of modern technology with a varied continuum of services;
- freedom from the throes of injury due to pollution of food, air, water, and the earth on which we dwell;
- the opportunity to grow, learn, choose, work, rest, play, be nourished, to experience well-being;
- solitude when needed;
- space, comfort, and beauty to discover him/herself;
- the power to improve his/her environment;
- justice;
- the dignity of risk, joy, and the growth of spirit;
- a valued social future.[3]

Use this creed as a basis for what your child specifically needs. Apply it to the various situations your child faces: school, vocational training, church, or residence.

ADVOCACY IN THE FAMILY

You will need to advocate for your child in your own family, both immediate and extended. You may need to advocate to your spouse about your child's behavior or school program. When you and your spouse are not in agreement, it may indicate that the family is not in a healthy state. In the extreme, one spouse may have to protect the child from the abuse of the other.

You may need to advocate to siblings about the child with special needs, educating other children about that child's needs and limits. This role is a healthy one, because you are guiding, instructing, and promoting understanding and love of one another. As the children grow, remain open about discussing the future needs of the child and make all of your children a part of the planning. Your advocacy now is a model for the role your other children may need to fill in the future.

You may have to educate extended family members—grandparents, aunts and uncles, cousins—about the child, as was discussed in an earlier chapter about telling others. The "telling" will probably go on for many years, as both the child and situations change. Sometimes members of your extended family do not recognize or understand the permanency of the disability. As this becomes apparent over time, you will need to continue to educate family members.

For example, learning disabilities are not well understood. Grandparents may try to be helpful by offering suggestions about how the child could improve study habits or how the child should show more effort. They may not understand why the child has the same problems year after year. The relationship of the child with the grandparents may be hampered because the child feels criticized by them, but they feel they are only trying to be helpful. A parent can mediate and intercede by explaining the disability or perhaps by providing reading material or arranging a conference in which the child's teacher can talk with the grandparents. Incidentally, your relationship with your parents may become strained because they may not approve of how you handle your child. If this is the case, you may want to find a counselor who would help you work through your misunderstandings.

ADVOCACY IN OUTSIDE SYSTEMS

You will also need to advocate with non-family people who provide services to the child. This advocacy will involve an interaction with several systems: the school, the community, the church, the medical community, as well as other service providers like the hair stylist or the bus driver. These systems are multi-layered. The layer you will interact with most often is the *direct-service providers,* such as teachers, doctors, respite-care workers, and case managers. Beyond the direct service providers are *administrators,* such as school principals and directors of agencies or clinics. The next layer is the *policy makers,* such as the school board and legislative bodies.

As an advocate, you will work with each layer differently. To be successful, you must recognize the divergent goals, strategies, levels of commitment, and purposes at each level. It's paradoxical that the direct-service providers, such as teachers, have both the most and the least power to make changes. A teacher, for example, has the most power over using strategies for changing your child's classroom behavior but the least power in changing the fact that he or she teaches twenty special-education students in one classroom, with no aide, which gives the teacher less time to concentrate on using those strategies with your child.

You may find yourself in the position of having to work at making system changes so that the direct-service providers can best help your child. You may need to band together with other parents to gather strength in changing the system. All systems are complex. Children will, throughout their lifetime, receive services from many agencies, with a variety of professionals who possess varying degrees of experience and training.[4] Knowing the system will give your child better access to services.

It was parents' efforts that led to the passing of P.L. 94-142. Parents banded together to demand school services for their children. Another piece of legislation that profoundly affects your child is the Americans with Disabilities Act (ADA), which gives those with disabilities rights of access. It literally opens doors and provides opportunities in living—in work and leisure—for all people with disabilities. However, parents of children with special needs will probably be the ones who will be responsible for enforcing the ADA. If you are not aware of what the ADA guarantees your child, write to get a copy of the document from your congressional representative or senator. Also send for the booklet "Questions and Answers About the ADA" from the U.S. Department of Justice, Civil Rights Division (see page 252 for address).

ADVOCACY AFTER SCHOOL YEARS

Another area of advocacy for this decade is for housing and vocational training for children with special needs. Although P.L. 94-142 guaranteed the right of all children to a free, appropriate education in the least restrictive environment, there are no guarantees for these children once they leave school. (Transition planning is now mandated under P.L.

101-46; see chapter 12.) Once the policy of deinstitutionalization took hold in this country, we recognized the rights of those with disabilities not to be institutionalized, but we did not provide a full range of alternatives. As a result, the majority of adults with disabilities remain with their parents, without vocational training, without employment, dependent on those parents. However, those parents will not live forever. Where are the guarantees for care for those who are dependent on others? Who will guarantee that these adults will have the rights presented in the "Children's Creed"?

The new era means that we parents now must turn our efforts toward another focus—the time beyond schooling, a time that will be a major part of the child's life. It's easy to become complacent during your child's school years, taking a breather because your child is in the right setting from September to May each year. It's also hard to see into the future. If your child is eight years old now, it's hard to be thinking about what your life and the child's life will be like in twenty years. But the years go quickly, and soon that eight-year-old will finish school, and you will be saying, "What now?"

ADVOCACY FOR THE FUTURE

Granted, not all school situations are perfect, but at least favorable laws are in place. Advocating with the school means insisting that the school complies with the law to provide an appropriate education for your child. Advocacy with the school may also occur on another level. For fifteen years we have been working out the kinks in special education. It's now time to move toward home-school collaboration to provide the best educational services for children.

Parents of young children with special needs must advocate

now for housing and vocational training, for their own children as well as for the children of the future. The advocacy for housing and vocational training must occur on the policy-making level. You will need to focus on making legislative bodies aware of the needs for specialized services. You may be able to profit from the experiences of those who were instrumental in passing P.L. 94-142, P.L. 101-46, and, more recently, the ADA. Advocacy requires getting the attention and ear of elected representatives to sponsor bills. With only six percent of introduced bills ever becoming law in a given session of Congress, the enormity of the task becomes apparent. However, it's only when programs have the force of legislation behind them that they become reality and available to all.

ADVOCACY IN AND BY THE CHURCH

Some would argue that Christian parents should not have to rely on the state to provide for their children. Theoretically, the argument may be valid. In times past, the church provided haven and refuge for those in need. However, churches today can't realistically provide for all needs. Churches can, however, play a role in providing both housing and vocational needs. For example, the Roman Catholic bishops of the United States issued a pastoral message, "A Century of Social Teaching," which marked the one-hundredth anniversary of the encyclical, "Rerum Novarum," the beginning of modern Catholic social teaching. Six themes were emphasized in this pastoral message:

- The life and dignity of the human person.
- The rights and responsibilities of the human person.
- The call to family, community, and tradition.
- The dignity of work and the rights of workers.

196

- The options for the poor and vulnerable.
- Solidarity.[5]

The pastoral message also proclaimed, "Parish life that does not reflect the Gospel call to charity and justice neglects an essential dimension of pastoral ministry. We cannot celebrate a faith we do not practice. We cannot proclaim a Gospel we do not live."

Celebration of faith and proclamation of the Gospel has applications beyond one particular denomination. If a church proclaims that it believes the Gospel, then it can't ignore the call of that Gospel to serve others. A specific example of living out this call is the many partnerships that have been formed by churches and local community agencies in building, furnishing, and staffing homes for adults with disabilities. In these partnerships the churches are, in a different form, living out the tradition of those religious orders of centuries past. These modern-day partnerships don't occur by chance. It's often an interested parent who will begin the process, planting seeds of interest by demonstrating need and sometimes becoming an active participant in the program.

I chose an example from the Catholic church because of its long history of teaching on social justice. However, many denominational and nondenominational churches have varied ministries to children and adults with special needs. In the Religion Division of the American Association of Mental Retardation an ecumenical spirit of ministry is evident. Ministers, pastors, and lay workers of all faiths come together at the annual convention to support and encourage one another, to share research, and to pray together for those whom they serve. It was while attending and speaking at an AAMR conference that I met Joni Eareckson Tada, founder of "Joni & Friends," which has a worldwide ministry to people with disabilities.

If you are not aware of national church committees and organizations that are concerned with people with disabilities, talk with your pastor or denominational leaders. Then contact those committees and organizations to see how they can aid you. Some denominations have residential housing facilities and special schools for children and adults with special needs. Some even have Christian-education materials that are written specifically for people with specials needs. Explore how you can use these materials in your church. Or if your church or denomination has not yet taken steps to address the needs of people with disabilities, research what other churches and denominations have done and share your findings with church leaders.

BECOME AN ADVOCATE

How do you become an effective advocate? The first step is probably acceptance of the role. Somehow it comes with the territory of having a child with special needs. Next is realizing that this role will not produce a miraculous cure for your child. No matter how hard you work, you can't change the nature of your child's disability by your efforts. What you will gain is better services for your child and others. A third step is to believe in yourself—your ability to learn, sort information, make decisions, and work with others to produce results. Fourth, you can make a decision to be a "participating family," that is, one who is active rather than only defensive in the system.[6]

Steps in Advocacy

Basic steps in advocacy include targeting, preparing, influencing, and following through.[7]

Targeting. Targeting is a two-step process: first identify the need; second, determine who can provide it. A basic needs assessment can be as simple as making a list of what a child needs in the coming school year for an IEP meeting. On the other hand, it can be as encompassing as participating in a large-scale, parent-group study of programs offered in a school system.

Once you target a need, determine who can meet the need. An existing agency may be able to solve your problem. If not, then you may need help from an organization or parent group to find out how to approach the person or agency that you think should be responsible for ameliorating the situation.

Preparation. Then do your homework. Get to know the system thoroughly. Before you take your proposed changes to a system, know your system. Who does what? Who is in charge of whom? Who has the power to make this decision?

Prepare yourself mentally for the meeting or series of meetings. Go with a positive attitude. Be determined to keep positive attitudes toward people, especially with those who provide direct services to your child. Smile, be friendly, and don't bring defensiveness or resentment into the meeting. If you need to make negative statements, make them in an assertive, nonaggressive manner that keeps the focus on issues and not individuals.

Be as familiar as possible with your rights and with legislation that affects your child. If you belong to a disability-related group, that organization usually will have a newsletter that will keep you apprised of information. Also, each state has a Protection and Advocacy Office that can provide information.

Influencing. The third step in advocating for your child is influencing decision makers. Developing good communication skills is essential in influencing others. You must make your statements clearly and then make sure the other person understands what you are trying to convey. You must also give feedback that indicates you understand the other person.

Organization is an essential skill in advocacy. Come to your meetings with a list of facts and accurately kept records to support them. Make sure the basic information is in a form that is easy for the other person to understand. Also keep accurate records of all of your interactions with others. Keep notes of phone conversations and meetings, indicating the names and positions of the people involved, the date of the interaction, the content of your conversation, including what promises were made. Keep copies of all correspondence. Make files of all your records.

Learn to ask specific questions and get specific answers. If someone tells you that something will occur, find out when, how it will happen, who will do it, and where the activity will occur. Make all of this information part of your file.

Follow-up. Most people don't realize the importance of follow-up. Once a person or agency agrees to provide a needed service, make sure that the agreement has been carried out. Periodically review the program or service to see that it continues to fulfill the agreement. If it doesn't, then begin the advocacy process again, targeting what now needs to be done.

In his book *Strategies: A Practical Guide for Dealing with Professionals and Human Service Systems,* Craig Shields lists sixty-nine specific strategies, organized by chapter headings, such as "Understanding Professionals" and "Knowing the System."[8] He gives a great deal of practical advice that is applicable to many different situations. For example: "If you suspect that a professional is bluffing, note the incident and go on, if the matter isn't serious. Later try and get at the truth. If the issue is serious, first try to encourage and allow the professional to change their position without losing face. If this doesn't work, challenge the professional, but try to keep the focus on facts and make sure you have your facts straight and well documented."[9] (If you can't find Shields's book in your library, you can order it from the address listed in the notes for this chapter.)

WHAT ABOUT SUPPORT GROUPS?

One of the problems I have faced is finding the right support group. Because my child doesn't have a disability that a large number of other children have, such as Down Syndrome or hearing impairment, I could find no support group that dealt specifically with Chris's disability. (Recently, I have found a Coffin-Lawry group, but the nearest member is 200 miles away. It is a relatively rare disorder.) Of course, the generic mental-retardation classification has a large national support network, the Association for Retarded Citizens. I've found that our state and local branches of the ARC have changed dramatically over the years. As many other disability-specific support groups have emerged, many that once were under the ARC umbrella are now on their own. As a result, some local and state ARC groups are defunct. You may have to form new organizations that include all disabilities, such as MUMS, Mothers United for Moral Support, which is a Wisconsin-based statewide support group for parents, grandparents, and professionals, encompassing children of any disability.[10]

ADVOCATING TOWARD THE IDEAL
OF COMMUNITY INTEGRATION

A concept that is of interest to most advocacy groups is community integration. The term can have a variety of meanings to different people, so it might be helpful to look at what the ideal would be like if ideal community integration existed.

- Services for children would be family based. All children, no matter what the disability, would be provided services as parents needed them, to keep the family whole. An alternative to remaining in the natural home would be placement with another family in the community.
- All adults would remain in the community and receive services necessary to live and work in the community.
- Professionals would be guided by persons with developmental disabilities and their families in design, implementation, and evaluation of services.
- Community members would be so committed to integration that segregated services would disappear. The community would work to ensure that all persons, both with and without disabilities, would participate in community life.[11]

The ideal may become reality one day if people with disabilities and their families, friends, and professionals join in advocating to make it happen.

PART IV

MAKING PEACE
WITH THE SITUATION

11

ACCEPTANCE
AND HOPE

As I sat down to fill in my outline for this chapter, I reflected on the words *acceptance* and *hope,* wondering if I should keep the chapter title. Some time had passed since my initial idea, and I wanted to be sure of what God was saying.

After reviewing my collected materials, the conviction was strong that the title should stand. That certainty came not only from reflecting on my own situation but also from reading results of research in which I am currently engaged. The topic of the research is the role of faith as a coping strategy for parents of children with disabilities. So far, almost thirty families have been personally interviewed about life with their children. The interviews have yielded a great deal of data, which are not yet fully compiled.

FAITH AS A COPING STRATEGY

When the research project began, I knew I wanted to incorporate the results into this book. Publishing deadlines did not allow time for formal data analysis, but the parents' statements included in this chapter will give you a good sense of the general response.

The focus of the research project is different from what other researchers chose to investigate in the past. I deliberately used the word "faith" as opposed to other variables, such as church membership, church attendance, or religiosity. In my life, what mattered in the clinches was basic faith—trust in God. When things got tough, I could talk with other people and I could go to church, but what counted was how I saw God and what part God played in my life. So I followed my own hunches in this study and focused on faith.

As I read the interview transcripts, I was so emotionally touched that I couldn't read them all at one sitting. At times I would be overwhelmed with what these parents had endured. I was often filled with admiration at the faith of these mothers and fathers.

The children in the study were of all ages, from less than a year to twenty-nine years old. The children had wide-ranging disabilities, including learning disabilities, hearing impairment, emotional disturbances, severe or profound retardation, rare genetic disorders, Down Syndrome, and others.

The parents' church affiliations also varied. Some had no church affiliation; others were members of mainline denominations or nondenominational churches. Their expressions of faith covered all types, from a simple, quiet trust in God to a more expressive, evangelical enthusiasm for witnessing or a charismatic orientation. Three of the fathers are ministers. No matter what the denomination or the type of faith expressed, I saw the threads of acceptance and then hope in all of these parents.

In fact, I began to wonder if I had asked the wrong question in my research. Instead of asking how faith is a coping strategy when dealing with a special-needs child, perhaps I should have asked how a special-needs child affects parents' faith. So many families experienced a strengthening of faith as the parents continued to deal with the problems surrounding the child. God became very real to these people in a way that had not been there before the child was born. I found, surprisingly, that many of the people were Christians. Some of the people interviewed were connected with the university where I teach, so I had about six known Christian families to begin with. But the majority were people with whom I had served on boards through the years or were from a list released by a city agency, and because of that, I was surprised to discover so many Christians.

Parents were asked to rate, on a scale of one to ten (one being lowest and ten being highest) the degree that faith was a coping skill for them. Eighty-three percent rated faith as seven or above. When asked to rate their ability to cope with their child's problems, eighty-six percent responded with a seven or above. A few respondents rated their faith as a coping skill relatively low but coping ability as high, and vice versa. As the data are subjected to more sophisticated analysis, more understanding of that phenomenon may come to light, such as the influence of the degree of disability of the child or the influence of support groups.

BIBLICAL ACCEPTANCE

Before sharing some of the statements of the parents in the study, I want to go back and discuss my original statement about acceptance and hope. As affirmation of the fitness of this title, I checked two of my favorite resources—the dictionary and Strong's concordance. The dictionary definitions of *accept* are

—to receive with consent,
—to give approval,
—to endure without protest,
—to regard as inevitable,
—to receive into the mind,
—to make a favorable response to,
—to undertake responsibility of,
—to receive favorably something offered.[1]

Acceptance is not passive. To accept a child is to reach out, to *give approval!* I was excited by these definitions because it described how my own relationship to Jesus Christ allowed me to accept my son. I could consent to him as he was. I could endure without protesting. I could make favorable responses to him. I could receive him favorably, as a gift from God.

This definition of acceptance relates to the definition of love in 1 Corinthians 13. If God's love can help me accept my son, then I can be patient, kind, protecting, trusting, hoping, and persevering. Trust in God, accept your child, love your child, and then hope.

Strong's concordance gives one listing for the word *acceptance* (there were many for accept and acceptable, but I wanted to concentrate on acceptance).[2] The passage is Isaiah 60:7, quoted here from the King James version: "All the flocks of Kedar shall be gathered together unto thee, the rams of Nebaioth shall minister unto thee: they shall come up with acceptance on mine altar, and I will glorify the house of my glory."

The word "acceptance" in this verse is translated from the

Hebrew word *ratson,* which means "delight, desire, favor, pleasure," and "voluntary will." That is, it is a voluntary act to find delight. In this instance, God finds delight in offerings, but in our situation, we chose to find delight in our children.

BIBLICAL HOPE

Webster's dictionary defines *hope* as "desire accompanied by expectation or belief in fulfillment."[3] In the Old Testament, the words *yachal* and *tiqvah* are often translated "hope." *Yachal* means "to be pained, to stay, tarry, trust," and "wait," as expressed in Psalm 130:5, 7: "I wait for the Lord, my soul waits, and in his word I put my hope. O Israel, put your hope in the Lord, for with the Lord is unfailing love and with him is full redemption." *Tiqvah* adds another feature of hope: expectation or the thing that I long for, as expressed in Psalm 71:5, "For you have been my hope, O Sovereign Lord, my confidence since my youth."

The New Testament makes dozens of references to hope, from the Greek root *elpo,* which means "to anticipate, usually with pleasure, expectation, or confidence." This meaning is seen in Titus 3:5–7: "He saved us through the washing of rebirth and renewal by the Holy Spirit, whom he poured out on us generously through Jesus Christ our Savior, so that, having been justified by his grace, we might become heirs having the hope of eternal life."

Acceptance and hope for Christians add a different shading to the picture of a child's disability. For me, it means that when things look hopeless or frustrating, I can focus on the long-range picture, the eternal. In the grander scheme of God's plan, the time we spend on earth is, indeed, brief. Corrie ten Boom once said that our lives are like a tapestry; God, the master needleworker, sees the picture unfolding on top, but we look at that tapestry only from the underside and see knots, tangles, and mere outlines of shapes. We have no idea of the beauty of the tapestry that we will see when we are with God.

When reading parents' statements in the interview transcripts, I could see that what set the Christian parents apart was their acceptance of their child in Christ and their eternal perspective of hope. Even though the parents who profess no faith may be coping very well, or even better than some who have faith, they do not express the same opinions about what part they and their children may have in an eternal sense.

When I first read the definition of the Greek root *elpo,* "to anticipate with pleasure and confidence," my heart took a small leap. Here was a new concept. Usually, I anticipate with dread the next fight for Chris's rights and services. Over the years I have been able to see hope take root in my heart. When I face a meeting, I now feel a sense of calm and almost resignation. I have confidence that God will work everything out for my son. I would like to get to "elpo," the point that I can anticipate these encounters with pleasure.

I like *elpo.* It means that I can anticipate the next meeting or the next decision as an event to look forward to, to watch how God is going to work. I can be more than resigned—I can be excited. If the perfect solution (in my estimation) is not reached, I can still rejoice because I know that God has a larger plan, that I'm looking at some knots and tangles but God sees the beautiful picture of Chris's life—a picture we'll see someday.

DAILY LIFE WITH JESUS

Hope doesn't run away from problems or deny that they exist. Many of the parents who said their faith was strong were also involved in volunteer and advocacy work for children and adults with disabilities. They kept themselves very well informed of rights, services, and options for their own child. Many are "fighters" with the systems in which they were involved and were adamant about the need to stand up for their own child and others. Being a Christian, accepting your child's special needs, and expecting God to work in your life are not antithetical to being an activist. The injunction to take up one's cross and follow Jesus does not imply passivity.

To pick up a cross, which is no light load, and then walk with it, means hard work. But Jesus' presence with us on the road makes the road bearable. As Jesus leads the way, he clears the road of potholes and land mines, and as long as we keep our eyes on him and his leadership, our path indeed will be straight.

I find that when I take my eyes from him and decide to travel on my own, I run into the obstacles and barriers. If working as a volunteer and advocate becomes an end in itself, you can find yourself becoming frustrated and discouraged. Forgetting the Lord of the work adds weight to the cross, until it becomes almost impossible to bear.

Jesus said that his yoke is easy and burden light (Matt. 11:30). If that's true, then, in Jesus, the cross is not meant to be heavy. For example, I once found myself in a volunteer situation that no longer interested me. When I finally took the time to ask myself what was going on, I realized that my service with that organization had come to an end. God had put me there for a time and a purpose, and then it was time to move on to do something else. Had I remained in the organization out of my own pride (I had seniority in the group), it would have been a continuing downward spiral of nonproductivity, I am certain.

PARENTS SPEAK OF HOPE AND ACCEPTANCE

As I read the parent responses to the research survey, I was encouraged by the strength the parents expressed. They told of their frustrations and disappointments, their acceptance and hope. I share excerpts from their responses in hopes that you also may be encouraged.

The Importance of Faith in Coping

Parents were asked, "How important is faith in coping with problems related to your child with a disability?" The following quotations express some of their responses:

Parents of a one-year-old child with Down Syndrome: "[Faith is] everything—100 percent. We're prepared by faith. Without faith I would see no reason for having a handicapped child. I could see no purpose. It's given us the opportunity to share Jesus and to provide hope."

Mother of a twenty-eight-year-old daughter with cerebral palsy: "I think [faith is] real important. You've got to believe in something. You've got to have some anchor somewhere. You just have to hope that this faith will give you the strength. Many times that's what you resort to, to help you get through things."

Mother who adopted a son with emotional problems: "[Faith is] pretty exceptional. We couldn't do it on our own strength. You couldn't make the decision in the first place to adopt a child on your own. You certainly couldn't handle it on your own."

Parents of a twenty-seven-year-old adopted daughter who is blind and severely retarded: "I don't think we could have coped without [faith]."

Mother of a twenty-seven-year-old son with Down Syndrome: "It's been a lot. If it wasn't for [my faith], I don't know how I'd do it alone sometimes."

Parents of a five-month-old son with cleft palate: [Father:] "I can't really figure out how people that don't know God could get through something like this because it's hard enough when you do know him. And yet, I know people get through, so I would be tempted to say that faith is indispensable, but people who don't know God get through it too somehow. [Mother:] On the other hand I think that in some ways, faith in God has made it more difficult than it would be if I just thought that everything that happened was random chance. I had to go through that struggle that God let this happen to my baby. You know, I have loved him and served him and given myself to him, and he let this happen to my baby. I wouldn't have had that struggle if I hadn't known God. [Father:] The other tension that our faith creates is that we believe in God's healing power for today, and we pray for people to be healed. For six or seven months we have been praying for our son to be healed, and it's just a little bit tough when it doesn't happen. We don't get discouraged and we don't stop praying and we don't question God, because he's sovereign, but still it creates a tension when you're always praying to see healing but never see it. [Mother:] Any peace we have is supernatural peace from God. The day-to-day circumstances are so trying that without the Lord, I would just be falling apart all the time. As it is, I fall apart only some of the time, and it's less and less of the time as it goes on, which is kind of encouraging when I look back."

Stepmother of two young adults with severe retardation: "[My faith is] very important. It's the only release."

Mother of an eleven-year-old son with spina bifida: "I attribute his healings to faith—different crises that have happened—miraculous healings. And because of it, I always

213

feel no matter what happens, we'll be okay. But there are still insecurities along the way."

Parents of two sons with Down Syndrome (a biological son, age seven, and an adopted son, age eighteen months): "[Our faith is] everything. It's foundational. Without that we wouldn't have a basis for hope."

From a mother of two daughters (ages six and nine) who have a rare genetic disorder: "Your belief system is what keeps you going, so if you choose to believe in God, he is what keeps you going. . . . We've met a lot of people, and that line about 'God knows who to give these kind of children to,' that's not true at all. . . . I think a lot of people mean it as if there's something really special about you, so he gave it to you. I don't even try to figure it out, because it's his plan, not mine. I think those people who think that there's some kind of strength that comes from within you—that whole mentality rubs me the wrong way. The person next to me very often could handle it, given God." (The six-year-old died a few weeks after the interview.)

In the interviews, three parents said that faith was not important in their life. One was the mother of an eleven-year-old son with cerebral palsy and many medical problems. She also has serious medical problems and indicated that she gave birth to this child only because her husband and his family pressured her into it. She does not attend church. She rated her coping ability as a five (average), with faith as a coping skill rated a two (very low).

A mother of a twenty-nine-year-old son with Mosaic Down Syndrome relates that two different ministers asked her not to bring her son to church because the child was offensive to the other parents. In her words, "I don't think I will ever be a part of an organized church again. I don't need that building to get me through life. . . . I've gotten more negatives from

214

ministers and doctors than from any educators or neighbors or anyone."

A mother of a twenty-one-year-old son with a learning disability, who is now obtaining his master's degree, said, "Although [faith] can be very important for some, for me it wasn't. We didn't have to rely on it." She rated faith as a coping skill as five (average), and her ability to cope as ten (highest possible).

Coping with Problems

We asked parents, "How have you coped with problems with your children?" Their responses were varied.

"[I was helped by] the support group and learning to be an advocate."

"I . . . have always been active in advocating for things. . . . We just had to change our lifestyle a little to accommodate our child. . . . We tried to do as many things as we could with the other [children]."

"You have to just cope. There's no choice. We refuse to spend life being bitter or whatever. It's pointless."

From the father of the same child, "Sometimes there are thoughts of what she might have to face, with others knowing that she's different. But a lot of that can be headed off at the pass. We make positive schemes—strategies for her. For example, to get her accepted, we thought of moving next to and joining a country club. . . . If we can get her accepted by the more prominent kids in the school, then she's likely to be accepted by the others. When she's school age, I plan to run for the school board. We consider them God-given plans. Also, having a secure family makes a difference."

"You just live with [the problems]. We use respite care to get away. It's only when I'm selfish that I think of it as a problem. I wouldn't change things, though."

"I have coped by becoming heavily involved in learning disability associations and special-education committees."

"In all that, the Lord gives you some special love for this child that you build your life around. You get to a point of acceptance, to a new level every month. He gives you grace to love this child, to turn it into something good, to help others. You must deal with it day in and day out. He supplies an inner peace. Sometimes I cope well. I look to him."

"[We cope] by communication between ourselves. Probably interactions with intimate brothers and sisters in the Lord. Prayer. Reading both Scripture and other informative materials. Probably to some degree trying to provide breaks for [my wife], time out."

"We just try common sense, that's about all you can do. I've tried to talk with [our son] and tell him that things have to be done differently at times. We just take time to explain to him, just talk to him."

"I have had to let [our son] take his licks, and he learns from his licks. It's not easy for me. . . . I have to trust God with his life all the time. We pray over him often and ask the Lord to watch over him. [My husband] is an incredible coping mechanism, since he's so knowledgeable regarding the laws, services available."

"[My husband] helps a lot. He has adjusted his schedule to be home as much as he can during the day to help [with the baby]. [A minister] would come to the hospital and just hang out while [our baby] was having surgery. . . . He'd say, 'Just don't be so hard on yourself, it's okay.' That was more helpful than you can possibly imagine, because I have all these expectations for myself. . . . It was real nice for him to say 'it's okay.' It had never occurred to me [that I didn't have to do everything]."

"I just cope with it . . . through sheer will power and

determination. . . . I cope with it also by attempting to focus in on what's good in [my son]. . . . He's a wonderful little boy. He has a good personality, a lot of love. He's bright. . . . It could be much worse."

"There was a mother's support group that I attended and that was very helpful. . . . You could go in there and scream and cry and yell, and everybody understood. You can't deal with it on a day-to-day basis because people don't understand what you're going through. They just look at you and say, 'They smeared your walls? Oh gross' and you think, *I'll lock the kid in the bathroom because I'm going to kill him if he comes out.*"

"Counseling . . . different support groups . . . classes . . . volunteer work. . . . I notice that I have more bad days now than I did when they were little, and I think once they reach school age and you have to always fight for services, it gets old, it gets hard. . . . Another way, I guess, of helping me cope is I teach her to do . . . things so that she can help me. . . . I'm not always going to be around for her, and I want her to be able to cope too. It takes a lot of patience, but it's important."

"You decide it's part of life. Work at how to change it, with doctors or treatments. The family adjusts. There's mediation, a lot of problem solving. It takes up your mind. I try to make things in the house more accessible, arrange activities so his friends will come here and play with him, and so he'll have a feeling of accomplishment. It's an effort for me."

"I think the best thing that's happened, and I've been going probably six years, is . . . the support group that I go to. We all have . . . terminally ill . . . severely handicapped children."

"I'm a self-help person. Very independent. I solve problems myself. I research it and find answers. I talk to those I need to and tell them based on research what I want to see. I attend workshops. I have been a parent advocate to answer questions of other parents and show them how to get what they're entitled to."

"We sought prayer from different churches. Assertiveness. Friends came out. . . . We called the 700 Club for prayer and just stood by his bedside and sang victory songs continuously. We watched his spirit come alive again."

"[We cope] by working a lot harder. We've sought services. Respite program and the school have been a big support to me. We're at a crisis point since school has ended [their child is twenty-two]. We're hoping city programs will be available. We've just sought out what's available to help us cope. A medical background has helped too. The combination of that and faith has been helpful in getting through."

"I've been able to cope since I've trusted the Lord to give me the strength. When I was remarried, we had five children, and all had to help take turns to care for [our special-needs child.] When [our child] left home to go to an educational residential facility, then I felt how much was taken off of me. I did what I had to do while in it."

"I call the special-education director and tell him what I need. . . . We refuse to sign the IEP without the changes; that always gets them. It puts the school in turmoil. We know [our son's] rights. We rewrote the IEP at one time. You need to work to make things better. We try to work with them though."

"I've used professionals to support me and guide me into how to deal with what [my son] needs. And I've used community services to provide outlets for my needs and for his needs to make sure that we both have as close to what can be a normal life as possible. I've sought out God and have worked on my own personal problems to be able to focus on what [my son] needs. . . . We have a moms' support group that I attend. . . . If there's anything out there that can be used, I've been sure to latch onto it."

"[We coped by taking life] one moment at a time. Sleep came later, when we got some care to come in. . . . So I was first of all able to get some sleep, because exhaustion is such an enemy. . . . I try not to look at the whole picture. God says I'm only asking you to deal with one thing. Wisdom comes with age, through experience."

"I prayed a lot. . . . I also have a best friend who has a son that's a month older. . . . We talk a lot, and I think that's helped, too. . . . I've counseled new parents, and I think that's helped me because I've had the opportunity to tell them of the good times and the bad times."

In each of these parents' statements, I can find fragments of my own story—the things I've been through and the emotions I've felt. For most of these parents, their faith is what keeps them going. Faith allows them to find healing in being a volunteer or advocate. Faith helps them to continue to rearrange their lives. Faith gives them strength to teach their children.

PRAISING GOD IN ALL CIRCUMSTANCES

I recently paged through Robert Schuller's *Living Positively One Day at a Time,* a devotional book I had read over ten years ago.[4] As I reviewed the book and the reflections that I wrote at the end of each chapter, I realized how instrumental that book had been in my life.

One devotional, "Play It Down and Pray It Up!" had as its Scripture reference Psalm 34:1, "I will praise the Lord no matter what happens. I will constantly speak of his glories and grace" (TLB). Dr. Schuller wrote about biblical characters who encountered tragedies and hurts and how God was faithful as they turned to him. For example, David in Psalm 57 chooses to praise God, even though Saul is pursuing him and threatening to kill him. Paul, in 2 Corinthians 1, is in trouble in Asia, yet he puts his hope in the one who will deliver him. Job, of course, lost everything, and yet he maintained trust in God, even praying for those friends who were of no help at all. Acts 16 shows Paul and Silas in jail, praying and singing hymns, although they had been flogged.

At the bottom of the page I wrote: "I choose to praise God, and I feel surrounded by his presence!"

As I paged through the book, I found that, on different days that year, I had decided that I could pursue a doctoral degree, that I could try to write a book, that I wanted to minister in some way to families of children with disabilities. On September 16, 1981, the reading referred to Philippians 4:13, "I can do all things through Christ who strengthens me." The "faith claim" I wrote at the bottom of the page that day was, "There will be a position created for me to serve." Actually, six years and a few months later, having obtained both a master's degree and a doctoral degree, a position was literally created, and I was asked to fill it. That position has been the launching pad for me. It has been through my university affiliation that I have been able to write, research, speak at conferences, counsel, and teach.

I had no idea years ago that all of these things would come to pass. I couldn't have imagined the turns that my life would take, no more than I can imagine what God will provide for my son, Chris. I can only continue to make faith claims—that God does indeed know Chris better than I do, that God loves Chris more than I ever could, and that God will provide for his needs in ways that I never could. Because I have accepted my circumstances and believe in God's acceptance of me, I can hope.

12

GETTING READY FOR THE NEXT STEP

When I held Chris in my arms for the first time, I could no more imagine today's circumstances than I could have predicted that the Berlin Wall would come down. Even when I received a diagnosis and lived through his early school years, I couldn't picture what it would be like for him to be twenty-five. It was only in the latter years of his schooling that I could clearly consider the future. The years since he has been out of school have flown by so quickly that it seems hard to remember those early days.

It's almost ironic that as I'm writing this chapter, I'm facing my own "What next?" Chris is nearing the end of his time at the residential training school, and I'm hoping to find a suitable placement for him in our community. The local agency that administers residences has assured me that Chris is at the top of the list, but I have no guarantee of placement.

Realistically, there are no guarantees for any of us, except that of eternal life together.

HOPE, NOT RESIGNATION

I'm facing the same situation that so many of you face: uncertainty about your child's future. I can approach the unknown from a different aspect now. When our youngest son, Shawn, was born, a priest came into my hospital room to inform me that he had baptized the baby during the night. He explained that the doctor would be coming in shortly to explain the situation to me and that it was routine procedure when a child had some problems. This had been a problem pregnancy, and, having one child with a disability, I had a sense of calm that was not Christ's peace but was a peace that came from resignation. The doctor came in and explained that Shawn's condition was not life-threatening, but it would take a week or so to resolve, and he predicted that all would then be well. I remember feeling almost numb, not even wanting to see the baby at that moment, deciding to wait until my husband came to visit that afternoon so that we would go see the baby together.

The first time I saw Shawn, he was hooked up to tubes, looking helpless and frail. I don't remember any feeling on my part at all. I concentrated all of my efforts on keeping calm. Happily, he is now a handsome, healthy, high-school senior, an honor student who is looking forward to pursuing a career in chemical engineering.

My sense of resignation, saying to God, "What next?" when Shawn was born is a direct contrast to the "What next?" I'm saying to God now that I'm facing a new situation with Chris. I didn't know God then as I know God now. With Shawn's birth, my resignation said, "Okay, God, heap it on. I've handled tougher things, and I can handle this one too if there is a problem." With the change in Chris's life, I now can say, "Thank you Lord for what you are going to provide for Chris in this new setting."

I'm not resigned to live under burdens that I perceive are sent by God, but I'm anticipating that God will work things out for Chris's best interests. A sense of adventure has entered into my own planning. My obligation is to do the ground work, the information gathering, and the compliance with whatever regulations are part of the process to move him forward to his next placement. However, as I do this, I wonder: "How is God going to put this one all together?"

DECISIONS FOR THE FUTURE

Each of you is at a different place in preparing for the next step. But no matter what age your child is, you have a next step to plan. Your child will continue to grow, and his or her needs will change. You as a family will change. If you have other children, their growing will affect your child with special needs. Family life doesn't just happen. Whether or not we are aware of it, we are always making decisions about our children's future.

Decisions made in haste or out of a tumultuous situation usually are not the best decisions. They are apt to be accompanied by a high degree of stress and may be followed by regret. Parents who are aware of what their child may be facing next and who decide to take time to plan are more likely to make better decisions, with more family members satisfied with the outcomes. Sometimes you avoid inquiring into the future or doing planning because you don't want to face reality. The reality is that things will happen with or without your planning. You can't stop time.

Someday you will die, whether or not you have made a will. Your child's days in school will come to an end, whether or not you have had a hand in planning what the child will do next. The child in infant-stimulation classes will be attending public school and will come under state and federal regulations, whether or not you are informed of the child's rights.

ELEMENTS IN DECISION MAKING

You will always face a certain amount of tension in planning your child's next step. Reflect on how the following elements influence your decision making.

You. The first element to consider is yourself. How willing are you to investigate, to look at possibilities, to recognize what work must be done? What is the quality of your faith? Are you keeping a healthy balance between relying on your own planning and trusting in God? What are your resources and priorities? For example, I may find a beautiful residence for Chris, but I may not have financial resources to keep him there. Or I may find a school or residential situation that is wonderful, and even have the money, but it may be so far away that I would see him only a few times a year.

Your child. What are your child's needs, strengths, and preferences? Children with medical problems require special consideration. Older or more articulate children will have more of a part in planning their future than those who are very young or who are not capable of understanding what is happening.

Your family. A third element in making decisions is your other family members—siblings, grandparents, perhaps even aunts and uncles. Siblings most likely will live longer than you will and may be connected with the special-needs child longer than anyone else in the family. Siblings should be a part of all planning as soon as they are old enough to understand. Your other children will have valuable insights on your child with special needs, and the information they have to give is valuable. I was discussing with my oldest son the plans that have been made for Chris when his parents are no longer alive. I was surprised to hear Jimmy say how important it was for him to be near Chris so that he could check on his care. The reason for my surprise was that Jimmy has lived away from home for over six years, ever since he went away to college. It would appear that because he feels confident that his parents are caring for Chris, he has no need to be actively involved at present. But his statement was a clear message to me that he would be actively involved when we were no longer around. This was new (and welcome) information for me.

Services and policies. When you make decisions about your child's future, consider the services or policies and regulations that affect your child. Much of this may seem out of your control: what is available today may not be there tomorrow; on the other hand, a gap in today's services may be filled tomorrow. Federal, state, and local budgets are always shifting. Keep abreast of legislative concerns through parent/advocacy organizations, and consider trends in your planning. Legislative changes are usually a slow process, but their progress is relatively easy to track. Program changes, however, can occur quickly. Staff changes are the rule rather than the exception in helping services.

Medical issues. As you plan for your child's future, look at what's being done in medical research. New technologies, new drugs, and the recent progress in genetics offer hope. What you may have never hoped to dream for your child may come true. Recently, several genes have been linked to specific diseases, including a type of deafness, several forms of cancer, Marfan's Syndrome (a growth disorder), cystic fibrosis, a type of Alzheimer's disease, and sickle-cell anemia.[1] Also, many surgical techniques now can correct conditions that were once thought to be permanently incurable. There is no reason to believe that such progress in medicine will not continue. Granted, some conditions will not be affected by drug therapy or surgery, and the condition will remain with the child. I don't believe that we will come to the point of being able to correct all existing conditions. But, with progress, hope exists for amelioration of many disorders and diseases.

God's love and grace. As you plan for your child's future, remember the tremendous resource available through God and his love, grace, wisdom, and guidance. The Bible gives you reason to hope and confidently anticipate your child's future. Gain strength and perspective from these words from Isaiah:

- "Seek the Lord while he may be found; call on him while he is near" (Isa. 55:6).
- "'For my thoughts are not your thoughts, neither are your ways my ways,' declares the Lord. 'As the heavens are higher than the earth, so are my ways higher than your ways and my thoughts than your thoughts'" (Isa. 55:8–9).
- "You will go out in joy and be led forth in peace; the mountains and hills will burst into song before you, and

226

all the trees of the field will clap their hands" (Isa. 55:12).

- "The Spirit of the Sovereign Lord is on me, because the Lord has anointed me to preach good news to the poor. He has sent me to bind up the brokenhearted, to proclaim freedom for the captives, and release from darkness for the prisoners, to proclaim the year of the Lord's favor and the day of vengeance of our God, to comfort all who mourn" (Isa. 61:1–2).
- "I delight greatly in the Lord; my soul rejoices in my God" (Isa. 61:10).
- "Yet, O Lord, you are our Father. We are the clay, you are the potter; we are all the work of your hand" (Isa. 64:8).

As these verses gave hope to God's people of freedom from their oppression, and hope of a Messiah yet to come, so they also comfort me. As God's promises were fulfilled in the Incarnation of Jesus, of God's love made flesh, for all of us, so I can believe that I have access to promises for my own children. It is all the more wondrous because I don't have access to knowledge of the mind of God. I must trust that God's ways are best, that the Master Potter will shape vessels according to his needs for their service, that he will care for those vessels of his grace.

FAMILY RESPONSIBILITY

President George Bush, when writing of issues regarding people with disabilities, stated a central issue succinctly, "But as important as government and community help is to integrating those with disabilities in American life, the family still remains in the center. . . . The key is to support—not supplant—the family."[2] You will have a central role in planning for your child's future. It is your responsibility to find the resources to help your child and to make the decisions that will affect your child's growth. Professionals recognize the value of family. In a paper describing an assessment procedure, the writer said, "Know that parental observations of their child's usual behaviors and skills often have greater validity than professionals' observations during the assessment. This should be reflected in the written assessment report."[3]

A parent can't rely on the school for all of the information necessary to plan. Your child probably will have a different teacher each year. While the teachers' observations are valuable, they aren't comprehensive because they are limited to only one setting. Gather information from the teacher, but then add your own understanding, judgment, wisdom, and discernment, which are all gifts of the Holy Spirit.

You will face some difficult decisions in the years ahead. Many will relate to teaching your child skills and knowledge that often are not addressed by schools:

- self-care, health habits, and first aid;
- how to avoid peer pressure in areas of legal and illegal addictive substances, such as tobacco, alcohol, and other drugs;
- knowledge about sexuality and marriage;
- knowledge about dating relationships;
- residence after school ends;
- work opportunities during and on completion of school.

Doris Richards wrote of how she and her husband made a decision regarding sterilization of their seventeen-year-old daughter, who has Down Syndrome. They felt that because she is mild-to-moderately retarded and has been educated, she would be in places where she would be exposed to the possibility of having a sexual encounter. The parents didn't approach this decision in a cavalier manner; they were aware of the painful moral judgment they were making. Doris said, "We felt that we had provided a measure of protection, even a certain amount of freedom, to a young woman who already has too many restrictions in her life. . . . I believe it is time society provided more leeway, freedom, equality, and assistance to . . . families when faced with an important decision such as this one."[4]

Unfortunately, freedom from pregnancy is not the only issue that adults with disabilities face. Freedom from abuse and from sexually transmitted diseases are two areas that parents can't control, except through education. Even with education, parents will have to live with some amount of uncertainty because they will not always be able to be with their children.

FEDERAL LEGISLATION AND FUTURE PLANNING

Although parents will remain crucial in planning for their children, recent federal legislation provides support for the future. The purpose of the Americans with Disabilities Act of 1990 is, "To provide a clear and comprehensive national mandate to end discrimination against individuals with disabilities; provide enforceable standards addressing discrimination against individuals with disabilities; and ensure that the Federal government plays a central role in enforcing these standards on behalf of individuals with disabilities."[5] The largest area of impact of the ADA will be in the workplace, where discrimination on the basis of disability is not allowed. In addition, transportation systems must be modified so that a person with a disability has a means to get to work. Also, obstacles and inconveniences will have to be removed so that people with disabilities can enjoy restaurants, movies, shopping, and other public places.

We can only hope that the removal of architectural and employment barriers is the beginning of the elimination of the attitudinal barrier for those with disabilities. It will take many years before our country becomes totally accessible.

Another federal law, P.L. 101-46, the Individuals with Disabilities Education Act (IDEA), requires that plans for transition from school be included in a student's IEP by the time the student reaches the age of sixteen. Although a student may remain in school until age twenty-two, the planning for transition must begin five years earlier.

Transition services include

- post-secondary education;
- vocational training;
- integrated employment, including supported employment;
- continuing and adult education;
- adult services;
- independent living;
- community participation.

Transition services are defined as, "A coordinated set of activities for a student, designed within an outcome-oriented process, which promotes movement from school to post-school activities," including those listed above. These activities "shall be based upon the individual student's needs, taking into account the student's preferences and interests, and shall include instruction, community experiences, the development of employment and other post-school adult living objectives, and, when appropriate, acquisition of daily living skills and functional vocational evaluation."[6]

According to the U.S. Department of Education, a 1990 study indicated that almost fifty percent of all students with disabilities left school with neither a diploma nor a certificate of completion. Almost two-thirds of all disabled Americans ages sixteen to twenty-four are not working.[7]

PARENTS AND TRANSITION PLANNING

You can join forces with school personnel in developing transition plans, even though the task may seem overwhelming. I remember that in Chris's last year of school, I was asked what I planned for him vocationally. The question boggled my mind, because my first reaction was to ask, "What are the possibilities?" Traditionally, one looks at what jobs are available and then sees if the job fits the individual. As it was Chris's last year in the school and the school's first year in using this approach, we didn't make much progress except to discuss possibilities in general terms.

The vocational-assessment process is much broader than the traditional approach to job hunting. It has many aspects, and parents can participate by contributing information to the process as well as by encouraging their son or daughter in vocational awareness. Information about the person to be included in vocational assessment should contain the following:

- awareness of career development;
- interests;
- aptitudes;
- special needs;
- learning styles;
- work habits and behaviors;
- personal and social skills;
- values and attitudes toward work;
- self-concept;
- work tolerances.[8]

231

While school personnel will be able to record observations, anecdotal information, on-the-job tryouts, classroom-performance samples, tests, and some of the information listed above, you can add your own observations and anecdotes about your child. Both you and the teacher will learn about your child through this process.

You can help your child in the vocational-assessment process by doing the following:

- Explore jobs in the local community. Take your child to various job sites of family and friends.
- Encourage independence in your child by assigning household chores.
- Take an active role in the development of the IEP so that your child has courses in prevocational areas, such as home economics and industrial arts.
- Request that your daughter or son be included in career-exploration activities in school, such as career days, class presentations, and career fairs.
- Suggest that career activities be included in your child's classroom, such as opportunities for an internship or supported employment.
- Try to arrange for your son or daughter to have a summer job, either with or without pay.
- Seek out your child's special-education teacher, the vocational-education director, or the guidance counselor to learn of opportunities.
- Inquire if a Curriculum-Based Vocational Assessment (CBVA) is in use in the school. If it is not, encourage its inclusion, perhaps by contacting the local Special-Education Advisory Committee and the Director of Special Education.
- Where CBVA is in use, make sure that this assessment takes place annually.

232

- Insist that CBVA findings are included in your child's IEP.

While our society is moving forward on mandated accessibility and vocational assessment, we still have a long way to go to ensure that all children will complete educational programs and have job and housing opportunities. The Association of Retarded Citizens points out that increased numbers of children are "aging out," that is, completing school eligibility and therefore having fewer legislative mandates apply to them. It is estimated that in 1987, one hundred thousand people with mental retardation were on waiting lists for residential services in communities. If those who were in institutions were included, the number would double.[9]

In 1990, Virginia Commonwealth University conducted an extensive statewide survey and stated that as many as sixty percent of older adults with developmental disabilities were unknown and unserved by state agencies; translated into numbers for just the Commonwealth of Virginia, that would equate to over thirty-five hundred adults in Virginia alone that were unserved.[10]

"NEXT STEPS" FOR ALL PARENTS

No matter how old your child is now, you can take some actions to begin the next steps.

- Keep abreast of legislation that affects the rights of your child and the development of new programs and initiatives. Do whatever you can so that needed legislation is passed.
- Stay in close contact with service providers in your own community. Volunteer as you are able to be part of a board or a committee. You not only will keep informed but also will have a voice in your community.

- Become aware of the steps you must take for financial planning for your child. The appendix has a list of some services in this area. Don't delay naming guardians, making a will, and beginning to plan a future because you or your children are young.
- Encourage independence in your child from the beginning. Allow your child to do as much for himself or herself as possible. Have an expectation that your child will achieve. Keep an open mind for options and possibilities. It takes longer to teach a skill and to supervise its development that it does to do a task for your child, but the rewards are greater in the long run. You will contribute significantly to your child's self-esteem by encouraging achievement in tasks both large and small.
- Teach your child the decision-making process. Allow choices whenever possible, even if those choices are from two options that you have introduced. When a child senses a parent's confidence, self-confidence follows, and the child's self-esteem is enhanced.
- When possible, teach your child to be a self-advocate. Encourage the child to speak up about needs and wants when appropriate in school or agency meetings.
- Hold out hope. I don't mean for that to be a simplistic statement. Hope is foundational to our Christian experience. Your faith in God doesn't guarantee you an easy life. But it does guarantee that God will walk with you through your difficult decisions and into the future.

WALK IN GOD'S SPIRIT

In closing this final chapter, I would like to draw from a brief but powerful book by Henri Nouwen, *Making All*

Things New.[11] The purpose of this book is to help people enter more deeply into the spiritual life. As his foundational passage, Nouwen chose Matthew 6:25–34, whose key words are "Don't worry."

Nouwen says we are so filled with worry that we are too busy to allow the Spirit of God to breathe freely in us and renew our lives. Nouwen says that Jesus is not telling us to pull away from things that are important and of value in our lives but to change our priorities: "Jesus wants us to move from the 'many things' to the 'one necessary thing.'"

This dynamic book points out that Jesus led a very busy life, but his life was marked by a central theme: to do his Father's will. This will was not autocratic. Rather, Jesus' obedience was a "total, fearless listening to his loving Father." God's love is caring yet demanding, supportive yet severe, gentle yet strong. We can tap into this love by accepting the truth of the divine life, which Nouwen says is "to enter into a divine betrothal." This process does not mean being lifted out of the world, but continuing Jesus' mission in our own worlds.

We can live the spiritual life by having a change of heart, a conversion. A few of Nouwen's sentences spoke strongly to me as the parent of a child with special needs:

> "All these other things," which so occupied and preoccupied us, now come as gifts or challenges that strengthen and deepen the new life which we have discovered. This does not mean that the spiritual life makes things easier or takes our struggles and pains away. The lives of Jesus' disciples clearly show that suffering does not diminish because of conversion. Sometimes it even becomes more intense. But our attention is no longer directed to the "more or less." What matters is to listen attentively to the Spirit and to go obediently where we are being led, whether to a joyful or a painful place.

Poverty, pain, struggle, anguish, agony, and even inner darkness may continue to be part of our experience. They may even be God's way of purifying us. But life is no longer boring, resentful, depressing, or lonely because we have come to know that everything that happens is part of our way to the house of the Father.[12]

I can't claim that life got easier for me once I came to know Jesus in a personal, real way. From my research with other parents, I learned that they also still face the same hard questions and choices regarding their children. But what I sense from them and what I can verify in myself is a deeper knowledge of God's peace, joy, and love—no matter what the circumstances.

The process is a gradual, lifelong one. I am further in all of this than I was ten years ago and not as far as I will be ten years from now. Salvation involves point-of-time conversion as well as lifelong moving toward God. I can now rejoice that having a child with special needs is part of my process of salvation. That is not the role I would ever have chosen, but I know that God can use it for good. My perspective includes not just what I see, but also what I can't see, beyond the lifetimes of myself and my son, into eternity.

As you have shared my life story, I feel that I, in writing, have shared in yours. I invite you to make a covenant with me to pray for all parents who will be reading this book, that they will find not only some practical assistance in helping their child but also a broader sense of God's love in their own lives, and in the lives of those they love, especially their very special children.

EPILOGUE

Some major events have occurred in my life since I completed the writing of this book. I finished the manuscript at the end of 1991; it is now June 1992. A place is opening for Chris in a group home in my community. It is not the ideal, small, family-care home that I feel will be best for him; but it is nearby, spacious, and modern, and it will be a residence for him for the next year or two until a family-care home is available.

The second major event is that I am very happily remarried. Chris was at our wedding and behaved beautifully. At the end of the ceremony we called all seven of our children to the front of the church to introduce them to the guests, and Chris gave the victory sign when applauded. He mingled with the guests, introduced himself to people he didn't know, and my female students told me that he complimented them on their outfits.

My youngest son is going off to college this fall, and for the first time, there will be no children at home. I will be adjusting to my newfound status as a free person. God has been good to me beyond all I could envision or deserve. For all that has happened in my life, I give thanks.

INFORMATION CHECKLIST FOR RESIDENTIAL SETTINGS

When you consider various residential settings for your child, use this checklist to gather information for evaluation.

- What are the names of all of the staff with whom my child would have contact?
- What are the specific assignments of each of the staff persons and the days/hours that each person works—specifically, who is day staff, who is night staff, and who is weekend staff?
- Who is the one person who has the most overall contact with and responsibility for my child?
- What is the best time of day to call that person if needed?
- What is the schedule for work, training, schooling, recreational activities?
- What specific skills would be helpful to my child before entering? (For example, I found that training Chris to recognize his own laundry label would have been very helpful.)
- Who will read mail to my child (if your child can't read)?
- What is the best time of day to call my child?

- Can my child call me? Will someone assist him or her in doing that?
- When are periodic reviews and assessments made of my child's program?
- Can I be a part of that assessment and planning?
- What is the best time of year to enroll? Will the vacations of staff affect my child's orientation and adjustment?
- Ask to see documentation of the residents' human rights.
- Be sure the facility is licensed.
- Inspect all areas, especially living and sleeping areas.
- What is the procedure for laundry and care of clothing?
- Are regular fire drills conducted, and are appropriate safety devices used such as smoke alarms and hot-water temperature regulators?
- What are the policies on home visits?
- What kinds of possessions are advisable to have, such as tape recorders, televisions, or radios? Look at rooms or apartments of others to get an idea of what is feasible.*

---

*From Rosemarie Scotti Cook, *Counseling Families of Children with Disabilities* (Dallas, Tex.: Word, 1990).

ORGANIZATIONS FOR PEOPLE WITH DISABILITIES AND THEIR FAMILIES

Advocates with Persons Who Are Developmentally Disabled (ADD)
P.O. Box 11148
Santa Ana, CA 92711

ADD is a group of Christians who believe that the church has a unique opportunity to minister to and with persons with developmental disabilities and their families.

ADD serves to provide community service, Christian education, and advocacy that include

- training for respite care to church groups and interested individuals.
- assistance in creating Christian homes for persons with disabilities.
- resources and networking information to families, churches and communities.
- assistance to churches in establishing church school classes.
- training for church school teachers, pastors, and others interested in sharing ministry with people with disabilities.

241

- raising church and community consciousness through newsletters, brochures, and public relations.
- promoting inclusion of persons with developmental disabilities into the life of the church.

American Association of Mental Retardation (AAMR)
1719 Kalorama Road, N.W.
Washington D.C. 20009
1-800-424-3688
Of interest to both parents and professionals, who may be members at two levels—active and associate. AAMR publishes a journal, newsletters, and hosts an annual convention. The Religion Division of the AAMR publishes "Dimensions of Faith and Congregational Ministries with Persons with Developmental Disabilities and Their Families," a bibliography and address listing of resources for clergy, laypersons, families, and service providers. Write to

American Association on Mental Retardation—
Religion Division
31 Alexander St.
Princeton, NJ 08542

Association for Retarded Citizens of the United States (ARC)
500 E. Border Street
Suite 300
Arlington, TX 76010
(817) 261-6003
Advocacy, information, referral services, and a newsletter. Membership fees vary with location.

Beach Center on Families and Disability
Bureau of Child Research
University of Kansas
3111 Haworth Hall
Lawrence, KS 66045
(913) 864-7600; (913) 864-5323 FAX

A rehabilitation, research, and training center, "devoted to support the inherent strength of families over the life span." Provides information and research materials, as well as annotations of publications and research.

Broken Wing Outreach
1515 East 66th St.
Minneapolis, MN 55423
(612) 866-0462
Provides Bible studies, retreats, and worship services.

Canadian Association for Mentally Retarded, Kinsmen National Institute, York University
4700 Keele St.
Kinsmen Bldg.
North York, Ontario M3J 1P3
(416) 661-9611
Although primarily founded to deal with mental retardation, these organizations now focus on individuals with a wide range of developmental disabilities.

Center for Children with Chronic Illness and Disability
Box 721, UMHC
Harvard Street at East River Road
Minneapolis, MN 55455
(612) 626-4032; (612) 624-3939 Voice/TDD
Committed to physical, psychological, and social development and competence of infants, children, and adolescents with chronic illness and disability. Gives training, research, and information to those with disabilities and their families, as well as to professionals and policymakers.

Committee on Disabilities Concern
Christian Reformed Church
2850 Kalamazoo Ave. S.E.
Grand Rapids, MI 49560
(616) 246-0837

Promotes full participation of persons with disabilities in church life. Services to church leaders, individuals, and families; Christian education materials for people with disabilities.

Coordinating Council for Handicapped Children
20 East Jackson Blvd., Suite 900
Chicago, IL 60604
(312) 939-3513

A coalition of parent and professional organizations that publish manuals, pamphlets, fact sheets, and newsletters.

Council for Exceptional Children (CEC)
1920 Association Drive
Reston, VA 22091
(703) 620-3660 voice/TDD; (703) 264-9494 FAX

CEC consists of special-education teachers, administrators, students, and support-service professionals, working together to improve education for children. A few of CEC's special-interest areas include: technology, special exceptionalities, giftedness, and administration of teacher education. Located in every state, CEC hosts conventions and conferences; publishes two journals—*Exceptional Children* and *Teaching Exceptional Children;* and offers library services for members.

Department for Family Support Services
The Kennedy Institute
2911 E. Biddle Street
Baltimore, MD 21213
(301) 550-9700

Provides family-centered, preventative programs to families and professionals who care for children with developmental disabilities or with special health-care needs in the home and community. Provides education, support groups, case management, and direct services.

Direct Link Referral Service
P.O. Box 1036

Solvang, CA 93464
(805) 688-1603
   A clearinghouse for organizations that provide services.

Faith and Light
R.R. #1
Joshua Cook Lane
Wellsleep, MA 02667
(508) 349-2514
   An international, ecumenical association for people with mental disabilities, their families, and friends. Those interested in starting a Faith and Light community can contact the national coordinator for charter, constitution, and community guidelines.

Joni & Friends
P.O. Box 3333
Agoura Hills, CA 91301
(818) 707-5664; (818) 707-7006 TDD
   Joni & Friends is a nonprofit Christian organization accelerating Christian ministry in the disability community. Publishes the "Joni & Friends Newsletter" and sponsors conferences and retreats. The founder, Joni Eareckson Tada, is the author of several inspirational books and speaks at conferences around the world.

National Apostolate with Mentally Retarded Persons (NAMRP)
P.O. Box 4711
Columbia, SC 29240
1-800-736-1280
   Publishes a quarterly journal and newsletters; holds annual conferences; encourages spiritual, mental, and physical development of persons with mental retardation; and offers support to families.

National Organization for Rare Disorders, Inc.
P.O. Box 8923
New Fairfield, CT 06812
(203) 746-6518

A nonprofit, voluntary agency that serves as a clearinghouse for information regarding rare disorders and a network to families who have members with similar disorders. Provides education, advocacy, and research about rare disorders and Orphan Diseases. Excellent information and newsletter.

**Parent Advocacy Coalition for Education Rights
(PACER Center)**
4826 Chicago Avenue South
Minneapolis, MN 55417
(612) 827-2966; (800) 53PACER in Minnesota.

A coalition of organizations founded on the concept of parents helping parents. The PACER Center publishes *Pacesetter*—a magazine by and for parents of children and young people with disabilities.

The Association for Persons with Severe Handicaps (TASH)
11201 Greenwood Avenue, N.
Seattle, WA 98133
(206) 361-8870 voice; 361-0113 TDD; (206) 361-9208 FAX

A membership organization including people with disabilities, families, professionals, and community members committed to: involvement and desegregation of communities; eradication of injustice; research; education; dissemination of information; legislation; litigation; and excellence in services.

**Working Organization for Retarded Children and
Adults, Inc. (WORC)**
28-08 Bayside Lane
Flushing, NY 11358
(718) 767-4075

WORC strives "to bring dignity and freedom to people with severe or profound mental retardations and developmental disabilities," by providing a structured "family" atmosphere in a residential community.

INFORMATION

Center on Human Policy
Syracuse University
200 Huntington Hall, 2nd floor
Syracuse, NY 13244-2340
(315) 443-3851
  The Center has developed a variety of reports and resources on the community integration of people with severe disabilities. The project makes these reports available for the cost of reproduction and postage.

"Connections"
National Center for Youth with Disability
University of Minnesota
Box 721, UMHC
Harvard Street at East River Road
Minneapolis, MN 55455
1-800-333-6293; (612) 626-2825
  A quarterly newsletter published by the Society for Adolescent Medicine at the Adolescent Health Program at the University of Minnesota; aimed at enabling full participation of youths in their communities.

National Information System (NIS) and the Clearinghouse for Infants with Disabilities and Life-Threatening Conditions
1-800-922-9234
  A computerized database of information regarding special services available to children (from birth to two years old) with

developmental disabilities and chronic illnesses and to infants with disabilities and life-threatening conditions. The organization provides free access to individuals with disabilities, parents, physicians, and other health professionals. The caller may be referred directly to the appropriate service, and periodic follow-ups are made to ensure appropriate referrals.

National Information System (NIS)—for Vietnam Veterans and Their Families
Center for Developmental Disabilities
National Information System
Benson Building, USC
Columbia, SC 29208
1-800-922-1107 x401 in SC;
1-800-922-9234 x401 elsewhere

A nationwide, computer-based information and referral system designed to help veterans' children with special needs; veterans' families in need of counseling and support services related to their children's disabilities; and the Agent Orange Class Assistance Program through support and outreach. Free information is available regarding resources in your state.

Research and Training Center
RRI/Portland State University
P.O. Box 751
Portland, OR 97207
(503) 725-4040
National Clearinghouse (800) 628-1696

BOOKS, VIDEOS, AND NEWSLETTERS

Children and Adolescents with Mental Illness: A Parents' Guide
This resource discusses stages parents go through in dealing with a child with mental illness; addresses topics like hospitalization, therapy/treatment, long-term planning, and medication. Order from:
Woodbine House
5615 Fisher's Lane
Rockville, MD 20852
1-800-843-7323

Flying Without Wings: Personal Reflections on Being Disabled
The autobiography of Arnold R. Beisser, M.D., describing his life as a person with quadriplegia (Doubleday, 1989).

How to Get Services by Being Assertive
A 100-page guide to developing advocacy, negotiation, and communication skills in order to more successfully attain services. Order from the Family Resource Center on Disabilities (address given below).

How to Organize an Effective Parent/Advocacy Group and Move Bureaucracies
A 130-page manual available through:

Family Resource Center on Disabilities
20 East Jackson, Room 900

Chicago, IL 60604
(312) 939-3513

Mother's Almanac II
This resource for parents of children age 6–12, written by nationally syndicated columnist Marguerite Kelly, includes topics such as communication, family customs, and relations with grandparents (Doubleday).

Strategies: A Practical Guide for Dealing with Professionals and Human Services Systems
Written by Craig V. Shields, order from:

Human Services Press
P.O. Box 421
Richmond Hill, Ontario
Canada L4C 4Y8

Spinal Network
A comprehensive resource book offering a variety of information for those with spinal-cord injuries, including information on recreation, travel, computers, media, sexuality, disability rights, financial assistance, medical considerations, and research connections. Order from:

Spinal Network
P.O. Box 4162
Boulder, CO 80306
1-800-338-5412

Support for Caregiving Families: Enabling Positive Adaptation to Disability
This resource, edited by George Singer and Larry K. Irvin, leads you through the goals, tactics, and techniques to assist families; practical model-demonstration projects; coping skills for families; identification of informal and formal supports; and creation of the parent-professional partnership necessary for effective, practical support. Order from:

BOOKS, VIDEOS, AND NEWSLETTERS

Paul H. Brooks Publishing Company
P.O. Box 10624
Baltimore, MD 21285
1-800-638-3775; (301) 337-9580 in MD

"The Impossible Takes a Little Longer"
  Stories of four highly accomplished, seriously disabled women
who share a determination and optimism. This work affirms the
potential of all disabled persons. Available on film or video for sale
or rental for high-school, college, and adult audiences. Order from:

Indiana University
Center for Media and Teaching Resources
Bloomington, IN 47405
(812) 855-8087

SPECIALIZED TOPICS

Adoption

Janet Marchese, the adoptive mother of a Down Syndrome child, T.J., offers a free service in White Plains, New York, matching Down Syndrome babies with couples waiting to adopt. Begun in 1977, she has found homes for over 1,650 children.

"Consumer Information Catalog"

A catalog of free and low-cost federal publications of consumer interest. For sales and books contact:

R. Woods
Consumer Information Center-W
P.O. Box 100
Pueblo, CO 81002

Estate Planning for the Disabled
955 West Center Avenue, Suite 12
P.O. Box 808
Manteca, CA 95336
(209) 239-7558; 1-800-448-1071

Americans with Disabilities Act (ADA)
U.S. Department of Justice
Civil Rights Division
Coordination and Review Section
P.O. Box 66118
Washington, D.C. 20035-6118

RESOURCES AND AIDS

Call Me Card
A telephone calling card enabling disabled children to call home, even if unable to use a pay phone; good only for calling home, therefore, it's useless if lost or stolen. Free from AT&T. Call 1-800-225-5288.

Dental Unit for the Disabled: The Sunbeam Dental Unit
An oral-hygiene device that enables quadriplegics, amputees, and other persons with limited or no arm movement to care for their teeth independently. Order from:

Northern Electric Company
P.O. Box 70
Highway 49 North
Hattiesburg, MS 39402
(601) 268-2880

IBM National Support Center for Persons with Disabilities
P.O. Box 2150
Atlanta, GA 30055
1-800-426-2133 (Voice/TDD)
Organized to help individuals and professionals learn how technology can improve the quality of life for persons who are

disabled. A toll-free number is available for information on how computers can assist individuals with disabilities. Written information is available explaining types of assisting devices or software available for specific disabilities.

Resource Catalogs

Laureate—Talking Software for Special Needs
110 East Spring Street
Winooski, VT 05404
1-800-562-6801 Mon.–Fri. 8–5 EST.
Software specifically designed for children and adults with special needs. Compatible with Apple and IBM.

"One Step Ahead—Thoughtfully Selected Products to Help with Baby . . . Every Step of the Way"
950 North Shore Drive
Lake Bluff, IL 60044
1-800-274-8440 24 hours a day, 7 days a week.
FAX 1-708-272-8509
1-800-950-5120 for questions regarding products or services

"The Specialists in Special Education"
James Stanfield Publishing Company
P.O. Box 41058-C
Santa Barbara, CA 93140
1-800-421-6534
A publication offering programs for teaching sexual education, work training, social skills, and daily living skills, including video programs on self-advocacy for persons with developmental disabilities.

"Toward Independence"
Attainment Company, Inc.
P.O. Box 93160
Verona, WI 53593
1-800-327-4269
   A catalog of contemporary products for people with disabilities.

"Very Special Catalogue"
JESANA Ltd.
P.O. Box 17
Irvington, NY 10533
1-800-443-4728 Mon.–Fri. 9–9.
   Toys and products for the developmentally and visually disabled.

Toy resource list for children with multiple disabilities
Committee on the Multihandicapped Blind Child
National Federation of the Blind of Ohio
Parents of Blind Children Division
(blind with no other disabilities)
1800 Johnson Street
Baltimore, MD 21230
(multiple handicapped blind)
1912 Tracy Road
Northwood, OH 43619
Or call Colleen Roth, Committee Chairperson (419) 666-6212
   List is geared to mental age of the child and offers suggestions for
children with physical and visual disabilities.

For more information on toys:

LEKOTEK
2100 Ridge Avenue
Evanston, IL 60201
(708) 328-0001

and:

USA Toy Library Associations
2520 Crawford
Evanston, IL 60201
(708) 864-3330

NOTES

Introduction

1. Jack Wiersma, "One Body, Bearing Burdens," *The Banner* (November 11, 1991): 10.
2. Rosemarie Scotti Cook, *Counseling Families of Children with Disabilities* (Dallas: Word, 1990).
3. Robert S. Eliot and D. L. Breo, *Is It Worth Dying For?* (New York: Bantam, 1984).
4. Cook, *Counseling Families of Children with Disabilities.*

Chapter 1: THE ROADS TO DIAGNOSIS

1. Diane Wilcox, "Heather's Story," *Exceptional Parent* 21, no. 2 (March 1991): 92–94.

Chapter 3: WHAT NEXT? THE CHANGES IN YOUR LIFE

1. Richard P. Olson and Joe H. Leonard, Jr., *Ministry with Families in Flux* (Louisville, Ky.: Westminster/John Knox Press, 1990), 141.

Chapter 5: PARENTS AND SIBLINGS

1. *Current Population Reports,* U.S. Bureau of the Census, series P-20, No. 437 and earlier reports; and unpublished data. Note: Statistics on mental retardation were devised by assessing three

persons per household, making one-third of all the population adults, two-thirds children, and three percent of those children.

2. Joyce Maynard, "Secret Splurge on Silk Undies Is No Sin," *Virginian-Pilot* and *Ledger-Star* (May 5, 1991): J3.

3. "Ethical Considerations in Prevention of Developmental Disabilities," Transcript of a workshop presented at the 1983 Virginia Mental Retardation/Developmental Disabilities Prevention Conference, Region Ten Community Services Board, Charlottesville, Va., 1984: 31, 33.

4. Thomas M. Skrtic, Jean Ann Summers, Mary Jane Brotherson, and Ann P. Turnbull, "Severely Handicapped Children and Their Brothers and Sisters," Jan Blacher, ed., *Severely Handicapped Young Children and Their Families* (Orlando, Fl.: Academic Press, 1984), 215–46.

5. Elizabeth Wein, "Wednesday's Child," *Sibling Information Network* newsletter, 5, no. 4, (1987): 7.

Chapter 6: THE SINGLE PARENT

1. If you would like more information on single parenting, consult the following books:

Gerald A. Hill, *Divorced Father* (White Hall, Va.: Betterway Publications, Inc., 1989).

James E. Lindemann and Sally J. Lindemann, *Growing Up Proud* (New York: Warner Books, 1988).

Virginia Watts Smith, *The Single Parent* (Old Tappan, N.J.: Revell, 1976).

Charlotte E. Thompson, M.D., *Raising a Handicapped Child* (New York: William Morrow and Company, 1986).

Thomas D. Yawkey and Georgianna M. Cornelius, eds., *The Single-Parent Family* (Lancaster, Pa.: Technomic, 1990).

Chapter 7: PARENTING INFANTS AND TODDLERS

1. Marilyn Segal, *In Time and with Love* (New York: New Market Press, 1988), 47.

2. Ibid.

3. Ibid.

4. French McConnaughey, "Your Baby's Development," in Karen Stray-Gundersen, ed., *Babies with Down Syndrome* (Kensington, Md.: Woodbine House, 1986).

5. *Webster's New Collegiate Dictionary* (Springfield, Ma.: G. & C. Merriam Company, 1981).

6. Carol Tingey-Michaelis, *Handicapped Infants and Children* (Austin, Tex.: PRO-ED, 1983).

7. "Family Support, Parents Respond," *Exceptional Parent* (April/May 1990): 14.

8. "Respite Care: A Gift of Time," *NICHCY News Digest* (National Information Center for Children and Youth with Handicaps) no. 12 (1989).

9. Debbie Messina, "When Parents of Impaired Step Out from Stress, Respite Home Steps In," *Virginian-Pilot* (September 24, 1990): D1, D4.

10. Lucy Schumer and Eileen Siminger, "Laura's Care Book," *Exceptional Parent* (March 1991): 86ff.

11. S. J. Cameron, L. A. Dobson, and D. M. Day, "Stress in Parents of Developmentally Delayed and Non-Delayed Preschool Children," *Canada's Mental Health* 39, no. 1 (March 1991): 13–17.

Chapter 8: YOUR CHILD AND SPECIAL EDUCATION

1. Marvin J. Fine, "Facilitating Home-School Relationships: A Family-Oriented Approach to Collaborative Consultation," *Journal of Educational and Psychological Consultation* 1, no. 2 (1990): 169–87.

2. The Robert Wood Johnson Foundation, *Serving Handicapped Children: A Special Report* (Princeton, N.J.: The Robert Wood Johnson Foundation, 1988).

3. Richard W. Vosler-Hunter, "Families and Professionals Working Together," *Aware* (Virginia Department for Children),

XIV, no. 7 (August 1990): 20–24 (reprinted from *Focal Point* [Fall 1989/Winter 1990]).

4. Deborah Berger, "Asthma Doesn't Have to Stop You," *Parade Magazine* (June 16, 1991): 14–15.

5. "Self-advocacy and the Individualized Education Plan," *The Pacesetter* (Minneapolis: Pacer Center, September 1990): 13.

6. "Mighty Casey Hits Homerun!" *The Ortho-Prosthetic Center Newsletter* 4 (Spring 1991).

7. William C. Adamson, "Helping Parents of Children with Learning Disabilities," *Journal of Learning Disabilities* 5, no. 6 (June/July 1972): 11–15.

8. "Basic Principles for Changing Children's Behavior," *NICHCY News Digest* (National Information Center for Children and Youth with Handicaps) no. 6, page 2.

9. "Supportive Parents for the Special Olympics Athlete," *Virginia Family Forum* (March/April, 1990).

Chapter 9: LIVING AWAY FROM HOME

1. Carol Moczygemba, "Was Placement the Right Decision?" *Exceptional Parent* 19, no. 6 (November/December 1989): 35–40.

2. Jana L. Raup and Jane E. Myers, "The Empty Nest Syndrome: Myth or Reality?" *Journal of Counseling and Development* 68 (November/December 1989): 180–83.

3. Marcia Routberg, *On Becoming a Special Parent* (Chicago: Parent-Professional Publications, 1986), 8–9.

Chapter 10: ADVOCATING FOR YOUR CHILD

1. *Webster's New Collegiate Dictionary*.

2. J. I. Rodale, *The Synonym Finder* (Emmaus, Pa.: Rodale Press, 1978), 29–30.

3. "Philosophy of Services for Children," a poster. Source unknown.

4. Audrey J. King, "Challenges Facing the Family," *Rehabilitation Digest* (Summer 1988): 3–6.
5. Jerry Filteau, "Catholics Urged to Take Up Social Teaching with New Urgency," *Catholic Virginian* (November 26, 1990).
6. Audrey J. King, "Challenges Facing the Family," 3–6.
7. Tony Appoloni, "Effective Advocacy: How to Be a Winner," *Exceptional Parent* (February 1985): 14–19.
8. Craig V. Shields, *Strategies: A Practical Guide for Dealing with Professionals and Human Service Systems*. Order this book from Human Services Press, P.O. Box 421, Richmond Hill, Ontario, Canada, L4C 4Y8.
9. Ibid., 109.
10. Contact this group at MUMS, 150 Custer Court, Green Bay, WI 54301.
11. Susan Neal, "Community Integration," *In Our Shoes* (published by Virginia Institute of Developmental Disabilities in Richmond, Va.) 2, no. 1 (Winter/Spring 1989).

Chapter 11: ACCEPTANCE AND HOPE

1. *Webster's New Collegiate Dictionary*.
2. James Strong, *Exhaustive Concordance of the Bible* (Nashville: Abingdon, 1890).
3. *Webster's New Collegiate Dictionary*.
4. Robert H. Schuller, *Living Positively One Day at a Time* (Garden Grove, Calif.: Crystal Cathedral).

Chapter 12: GETTING READY FOR THE NEXT STEP

1. "Scientists ID Gene of Early Deafness," *Virginian-Pilot* and *Ledger-Star* (October 6, 1991).
2. "President Bush's Agenda," *Exceptional Parent* (May/June 1989): 21.
3. Audrey Leviton, Mary Mueller, and Cynthia Kauffman, "The Family-Centered Catalytic Consultation Model: Practical Applications for Professionals," unpublished paper, Department

for Family Support Services, Kennedy Institute, Baltimore, Md.

4. Doris Richards, "Sterilization: Can Parents Decide?" *Exceptional Parent* (April 1986): 40–41.

5. From an information statement, unpublished, undated, from Senator Tom Harkin of Iowa.

6. *NICHCY Transition Summary* (National Information Center for Children and Youth with Handicaps) no. 6 (December 1990).

7. Ibid.

8. Ibid., 2.

9. V. K. "Warren" Tashjian and Alan Abeson, "The ARC of the United States: The Waiting List Crisis," *Exceptional Parent* (March 1988): 58–59.

10. Bob Willis, "What Happens When the Caregiver Is Gone?" *Catholic Virginian* (September 2, 1991): 5.

11. Henri Nouwen, *Making All Things New* (San Francisco: Harper & Row, 1981).

12. Ibid., 58–59.

INDEX

INDEX

sleeping problems of, 25
special education of, 74–75, 161, 162
as a toddler, 134–36, 137, 143, 145–46
toilet training of, 134
uncertainty about, 23–24
vocational assessment and, 231
walking and, 25, 128–29
Christian schools, 167–68
Chronic sorrow, 70–71, 97–98
Church, 151–52
advocacy and, 193, 196–98
changes in perception of, 60
nurseries of, 142–43
Clearinghouse for Infants with Disabilities and Life-Threatening Conditions, 247–48
Cleft palate, 213, 214
CLF (Community Living Facility), 180
Cline, Sheridan, 142
Coffin-Lawry Syndrome, 32, 201
Commander parenting style, 100–101, 103, 106
Committee on Disabilities Concern, 243–44
Communication
with commander parents, 100–101
with dynamic parents, 102
with entertainer parents, 101–2
with getaway parents, 100
with infants, 129
in marriage, 84
with toddlers, 135–36
with victim parents, 101
Community integration, 202
Community Living Facility (CLF), 180

Community Residential Alternative (CRA), 180, 181
Community services, 66, 170, 175
Confusion, 69
"Connections," 247
Consumer Information Catalog, 252
Coordinating Council for Handicapped Children, 244
Coping, 215–19
faith and, 206–7, 212–15, 219
Council for Exceptional Children (CEC), 180, 244
Counseling Families of Children with Disabilities (Cook), 15
CRA (Community Residential Alternative), 180, 181
Crises, 87–91, 184
Curriculum-Based Vocational Assessment (CBVA), 232–33
Custody issues, 92, 107, 116–18, 120
Cystic fibrosis, 226

Dating, 228
David, 220
Deafness, 25, 226. *See also* Hearing impairment
Death of parents, 184, 224
Decision making, 223–27
Deinstitutionalization, 169, 195
Denial, 22, 23, 24–28, 31, 47
Department for Family Support Services, 244
Developmental stages, 132
Devereaux School, 53–54, 62, 172–74
Diagnosis, 19–35
change in impact of, 54–58
denial and, 22, 23, 24–28, 31

265

INDEX

expectations and, 162, 163–64

IEP in, See Individualized Education Plan

parental attitudes about, 156–59

parental motivation in, 162

parental responsibility in, 155–56

parental support in, 166–67

post-secondary, 230

in preschools, 139–40

residential programs and, 181, 182

success stories in, 161–62

The Specialists in Special Education, 255

Special Olympics, 66, 70, 129, 161, 166

Speech impairments, 157–58

Speech therapy, 133, 154

Speileberg, Susan, 87–88

Spina bifida, 12, 213–14

Spinal Network, 250

Spouse, See Marriage

Stepparents, 92

"Stop! Look! Listen!" technique, 164–65

Strategies: A Practical Guide for Dealing with Professionals and Human Service Systems, 200–201, 250

Stress, 45, 88, 115

in infants, 131

Summer camp, 183

Sunbeam Dental Unit, 253

Support, 49

Supported Living Arrangements (SLA), 181

Support for Caregiving Families: Enabling Positive Adaptation to Disability, 250

Support groups, 111, 201, 218–19

Survival Guide for People Who Have Handicaps (Gordon), 147

Tada, Joni Eareckson, 197

TASH (The Association for Persons with Severe Handicaps), 246

Teachers, 66, 157, 158, 165–66, 193, 228

Telling the story, See Explaining

ten Boom, Corrie, 209–10

Tests, 158, 188

Time out, 165

Tingey-Michaelis, Carol, 136

Tobacco use, 228

Toddlers, 134–52

church nurseries and, 142–43

communication with, 135–36

diagnosis and, 139–40

discipline of, 136–38

everyday concerns about, 138–39

parental roles and, 140

preschools for, 139–40, 143–45

self-care for parents of, 147–49

Toilet training, 134, 138

"Toward Independence," 256

Toy resource list, 256

Transition planning

legislation for, 229–31

parental role in, 231–33

Transportation systems, 229

Trust

in God, 46

in marriage, 84, 85

USA Toy Library Associations, 256

Velcro, 139

271